DATE DUE

# Antibiotics

# Other Books of Related Interest:

## Opposing Viewpoints Series

Alternative Medicine

The Pharmaceutical Industry

Resurgent Diseases

## At Issue Series

Do Infectious Diseases Pose a Threat?

Cancer

## Current Controversies Series

Alternative Therapies

Vaccines

"Congress shall make no law ... abridging the freedom of speech, or of the press."

*First Amendment to the U.S. Constitution*

The basic foundation of our democracy is the First Amendment guarantee of freedom of expression. The *Opposing Viewpoints* series is dedicated to the concept of this basic freedom and the idea that it is more important to practice it than to enshrine it.

OPPOSING
VIEWPOINTS®
SERIES

# Antibiotics

*Noah Berlatsky, Book Editor*

**GREENHAVEN PRESS**
*A part of Gale, Cengage Learning*

GALE
CENGAGE Learning™

Detroit • New York • San Francisco • New Haven, Conn • Waterville, Maine • London

Christine Nasso, *Publisher*
Elizabeth Des Chenes, *Managing Editor*

© 2011 Greenhaven Press, a part of Gale, Cengage Learning

Gale and Greenhaven Press are registered trademarks used herein under license.

*For more information, contact:*
Greenhaven Press
27500 Drake Rd.
Farmington Hills, MI 48331-3535
Or you can visit our Internet site at gale.cengage.com

For product information and technology assistance, contact us at

Gale Customer Support, 1-800-877-4253
For permission to use material from this text or product, submit all requests online at www.cengage.com/permissions

Further permissions questions can be emailed to permissionrequest@cengage.com

Articles in Greenhaven Press anthologies are often edited for length to meet page requirements. In addition, original titles of these works are changed to clearly present the main thesis and to explicitly indicate the author's opinion. Every effort is made to ensure that Greenhaven Press accurately reflects the original intent of the authors. Every effort has been made to trace the owners of copyrighted material.

Cover image copyright John Foxx/Stockbyte/Getty Images.

LIBRARY OF CONGRESS CATALOGING-IN-PUBLICATION DATA

Antibiotics / Noah Berlatsky, book editor.
    p. cm. -- (Opposing viewpoints)
    Includes bibliographical references and index.
    ISBN 978-0-7377-5209-0 (hardcover) -- ISBN 978-0-7377-5210-6 (pbk.)
    1. Antibiotics--Popular works. I. Berlatsky, Noah.
    RM267.A5212 2011
    615'.329--dc22
                                                        2010024434

Printed in the United States of America
1 2 3 4 5 6 7 14 13 12 11 10

# Contents

## Chapter 3: How Should Antibiotics Be Used to Combat Different Diseases?

## Chapter 4: What Are Some of the Dangers of Using Antibiotics?

# Why Consider Opposing Viewpoints?

> "The only way in which a human being can make some approach to knowing the whole of a subject is by hearing what can be said about it by persons of every variety of opinion and studying all modes in which it can be looked at by every character of mind. No wise man ever acquired his wisdom in any mode but this."
>
> *John Stuart Mill*

In our media-intensive culture it is not difficult to find differing opinions. Thousands of newspapers and magazines and dozens of radio and television talk shows resound with differing points of view. The difficulty lies in deciding which opinion to agree with and which "experts" seem the most credible. The more inundated we become with differing opinions and claims, the more essential it is to hone critical reading and thinking skills to evaluate these ideas. *Opposing Viewpoints* books address this problem directly by presenting stimulating debates that can be used to enhance and teach these skills. The varied opinions contained in each book examine many different aspects of a single issue. While examining these conveniently edited opposing views, readers can develop critical thinking skills such as the ability to compare and contrast authors' credibility, facts, argumentation styles, use of persuasive techniques, and other stylistic tools. In short, the *Opposing Viewpoints* Series is an ideal way to attain the higher-level thinking and reading skills so essential in a culture of diverse and contradictory opinions.

In addition to providing a tool for critical thinking, *Opposing Viewpoints* books challenge readers to question their own strongly held opinions and assumptions. Most people form their opinions on the basis of upbringing, peer pressure, and personal, cultural, or professional bias. By reading carefully balanced opposing views, readers must directly confront new ideas as well as the opinions of those with whom they disagree. This is not to argue simplistically that everyone who reads opposing views will—or should—change his or her opinion. Instead, the series enhances readers' understanding of their own views by encouraging confrontation with opposing ideas. Careful examination of others' views can lead to the readers' understanding of the logical inconsistencies in their own opinions, perspective on why they hold an opinion, and the consideration of the possibility that their opinion requires further evaluation.

## Evaluating Other Opinions

To ensure that this type of examination occurs, *Opposing Viewpoints* books present all types of opinions. Prominent spokespeople on different sides of each issue as well as well-known professionals from many disciplines challenge the reader. An additional goal of the series is to provide a forum for other, less known, or even unpopular viewpoints. The opinion of an ordinary person who has had to make the decision to cut off life support from a terminally ill relative, for example, may be just as valuable and provide just as much insight as a medical ethicist's professional opinion. The editors have two additional purposes in including these less known views. One, the editors encourage readers to respect others' opinions—even when not enhanced by professional credibility. It is only by reading or listening to and objectively evaluating others' ideas that one can determine whether they are worthy of consideration. Two, the inclusion of such viewpoints encourages the important critical thinking skill of objectively evaluating an author's credentials and bias. This evaluation will illuminate an author's reasons for taking a particular stance on an issue and will aid in readers' evaluation of the author's ideas.

It is our hope that these books will give readers a deeper understanding of the issues debated and an appreciation of the complexity of even seemingly simple issues when good and honest people disagree. This awareness is particularly important in a democratic society such as ours in which people enter into public debate to determine the common good. Those with whom one disagrees should not be regarded as enemies but rather as people whose views deserve careful examination and may shed light on one's own.

Thomas Jefferson once said that "difference of opinion leads to inquiry, and inquiry to truth." Jefferson, a broadly educated man, argued that "if a nation expects to be ignorant and free . . . it expects what never was and never will be." As individuals and as a nation, it is imperative that we consider the opinions of others and examine them with skill and discernment. The *Opposing Viewpoints* Series is intended to help readers achieve this goal.

*David L. Bender and Bruno Leone,*
*Founders*

# Introduction

*"I have been trying to point out that in our lives chance may have an astonishing influence and, if I may offer advice to the young laboratory worker, it would be this—never to neglect an extraordinary appearance or happening."*

—Alexander Fleming,
the discoverer of penicillin

Before the discovery of antibiotics, bacterial infections were largely untreatable. "*Streptococcus pyogenes* caused half of all post-birth deaths and was a major cause of death from burns. *Staphylococcus aureus* was fatal in 80 percent of infected wounds and the tuberculosis and pneumonia bacteria were famous killers," according to the article "Antibiotics, 1928–2000" on the Real Millennium Bugs: Immune to Antibiotics Web site published by the Australian Broadcasting Corporation. Before antibiotics, the "case fatality rate [of pneumonia] was estimated to be between 30% and 40%," according to Adam J. Ratner and Jeffrey N. Weiser in a September 1, 2006, article in the *Journal of Clinical Investigation*.

All of this began to change radically in 1928, when British bacteriologist Sir Alexander Fleming noticed some mold growing in a culture of *Staphylococcus* bacteria. He further saw that bacteria close to the mold appeared to be dissolving. Investigating further, Fleming isolated the bacteria-killing substance produced by the mold and called it penicillin. As Mary Bellis notes in her article "The History of Penicillin," a year after Fleming first saw the mold, he "published the results of his investigations, noting that his discovery might have therapeutic value if it could be produced in quantity."

Though Fleming recognized the potential of his accidental discovery, it took some time before the benefits were realized. In fact, as BBC News reported on October 8, 1999, "it was not until the early 1940s that its true potential was acknowledged and large scale fermentation processes were developed for the production of antibiotics."

Howard Florey and Norman Heatley of Oxford University came to the United States during World War II and finally developed a method for increasing the growth rate of molds by pumping air into vats of nonalcoholic corn liquor. After an extensive search for molds, they found that the one that produced the most penicillin came from, in Heatley's words (as quoted by Charles Grossman in an article on the Web site of Physicians for Social Responsibilty), "an overripe, moldy cantaloupe" he bought from a street market in Peoria, Illinois. In the same article, Grossman notes that penicillin production increased rapidly: "In the first 5 months of 1943, 400 million units of penicillin were produced. In the next 7 months, 20.5 billion units were produced. . . . By August 1945, 650 billion units were distributed each month."

The discovery of penicillin had a major effect on the treatment of infections. For example, "During World War I, death rate from pneumonia in the American Army totaled 18%. In World War II, it fell to less than 1%," according to the article "Penicillin, the Wonder Drug" on the Web site of the Botany Department at the University of Hawai'i at Manoa. The same article notes, "In addition to pneumonia and blood poisoning, the major causes of death, in hospitals, during the war, strep throat, scarlet fever, diphtheria, syphilis, gonorrhea, meningitis, tonsillitis, rheumatic fever, and many other diseases were successfully treated with penicillin."

Penicillin was so effective that it led to a serious search for other antibiotics. Most of the new antibiotics did not come from mold but rather from actinomycetes, a family of soil-dwelling microbes that have some characteristics of bacteria and some characteristics of fungi. The actinomycetes have produced "a variety of antibiotics including streptomycin, aureomycin, terramycin, and chloromycetin," according to the article "Medicine from Dirt" on the Web site of the Chemical Heritage Foundation.

Some of these newer antibiotics were effective against bacteria unaffected by penicillin. For example, Selman A. Waksman of Rutgers University made an important discovery when a local farmer told him that some of his chickens were becoming sick after eating contaminated soil. The soil turned out to contain actinomycetes, and Waksman isolated streptomycin, the first antibiotic that could fight the deadly tuberculosis bacteria, from them in 1943.

As Waksman's story suggests, in the early years after the discovery of penicillin, scientists developed many antibiotics relatively quickly. However, even more antibiotics were needed. The problem, according to the 2003 article "History of the Development of Antibiotics" in *World of Microbiology and Immunology*, is that "some bacteria do acquire resistance to antibiotics, so there is a continuous search for new and effective antibacterial agents." For example, as Matthew Herper reported in a July 11, 2003, article in *Forbes*, in 1977, Michael Jacobs "documented the first cases of resistance of *Streptococcus pneumoniae*, a common cause of pneumonia [and] ear and sinus infections, to several classes of antibiotics." Doctors still use amoxicillin against this bacteria, but over the last twenty-five years, the dosage prescribed has quadrupled as *Streptococcus pneumoniae* has become more and more resistant.

This book discusses the many uses of antibiotics and the developing dangers as bacteria gain resistance to them in the following chapters: What Issues Arise in the Prescription of Antibiotics? How Should Antibiotics Be Used in Agriculture? How Should Antibiotics Be Used to Combat Different Diseases? and What Are Some of the Dangers of Using Antibiotics? The viewpoints take different positions on how to use and safeguard antibiotics, but all agree that eighty years after the discovery of antibiotics, they remain some of the most important medicines doctors and patients have available to them.

OPPOSING
VIEWPOINTS®
SERIES

# CHAPTER 1

# What Issues Arise in the Prescription of Antibiotics?

# Chapter Preface

One of the most important factors a doctor needs to take into account when prescribing an antibiotic is the possibility of an allergic reaction. Antibiotic allergies are widespread—in fact, staff members of the Mayo Clinic state that an allergy to the antibiotic penicillin "is the most common drug allergy."

Still, antibiotic allergies may not be as widespread in practice as they sometimes appear. For example, 10 percent of people claim to have an allergy to the common antibiotic penicillin. "However, about 90 percent of people who believe they are allergic can take penicillin without a problem," wrote Roland Solensky in an article on the medical Web site UpTo Date, last updated July 13, 2009. According to Solensky, people often become less allergic to penicillin over time, so only about 20 percent of those who have had an allergic reaction will still be allergic ten years later, as long as they are not exposed to the antibiotic again during that time.

Many people experience rashes when taking antibiotics, but these adverse reactions are not necessarily true allergies. In a post on the Web site of *Parents* magazine, Dr. Alan Greene notes that the common antibiotics amoxicillin and ampicillin "can typically cause a red rash up to one week after taking them"; however, this rash is generally a side effect rather than an allergy.

Actual allergic reactions to antibiotics can include hives, rash, itchy skin, wheezing, and swollen lips or tongue, according to the Mayo Clinic's Web site. Rarer allergic reactions include Stevens-Johnson Syndrome, or SJS, which "typically begins with flu-like symptoms, followed by a painful red or purplish rash that spreads and blisters, leading . . . the top layer of skin to die and shed," according to a February 17, 2010, article on the Johns Hopkins Children's Center Web site.

The most dangerous allergic reaction, however, is anaphylaxis, a severe multisystem reaction. Such reactions can include difficulty breathing, a drop in blood pressure, swelling of the tongue and throat, or dizziness.

Among the antibiotics most often linked to allergic reactions are cephalosporins, ciprofloxacin, nitrofurantoin, penicillin, sulfonamides, tetracycline, and vancomycin, according to the article "Allergic Reactions" on the Web site PDRhealth. In all cases, the American Academy of Allergy Asthma & Immunology recommends that "if you suspect a drug allergy has occurred, call your physician. If your symptoms are severe, seek medical help immediately."

The viewpoints in this chapter will look at other issues that arise in the prescription of antibiotics.

> "Not finishing a course of antibiotics or using leftovers for subsequent illnesses means Americans are not getting the full dosage needed to completely kill a bacterial infection."

# Antibiotics Are Dangerous When Not Used as Prescribed

*PR Newswire*

*PR Newswire is a leading global vendor in information and news distribution services for professional communicators. In the following viewpoint, the author(s) report on a survey that indicates Americans do not often take prescription drugs—specifically antibiotics—as directed by doctors. The article states that this can be dangerous because it can cause bacteria to develop resistances. The survey contends that patients stop taking the antibiotics because they start to feel better, but this action results in not receiving the full dosage needed to completely kill the bacterial infection.*

PR Newswire, "To Use or Not to Use: Consumers Conflicted About Antibiotic Use; National Survey Shows Improper Use, Yet Concern over the Consequences," February 6, 2003. Reproduced by permission.

As you read, consider the following questions:

1. What educational initiative has the Council for Affordable Quality Healthcare (CAQH) launched to help educate consumers about the appropriate use of antibiotics?

2. According to the survey, how many Americans have stopped taking an antibiotic before finishing the prescribed amount?

3. What percentage of Americans who did not finish their medication saved the leftover antibiotics for the next time they are ill?

When the sniffles and cough strike this season, many Americans believe an antibiotic prescription will provide the quick cure. According to a new survey by the Council for Affordable Quality Healthcare (CAQH), a not-for-profit alliance of America's leading health plans and networks, one third of people have taken an antibiotic for a cold or flu, and nearly that many mistakenly believe that antibiotics are effective for these viral illnesses.

Using antibiotics inappropriately can cause devastating consequences because bacteria begin to develop resistance to these life-saving drugs. According to the World Health Organization, two Americans die each hour from infections caused by antibiotic-resistant bacteria.

To help educate consumers about the appropriate use of antibiotics and raise awareness of the growing threat of antibiotic resistance, CAQH, in partnership with the Centers for Disease Control and Prevention (CDC), has launched an education initiative called Save Antibiotic Strength (SAS) in New York, Connecticut, New Jersey, Pennsylvania, Georgia, Norfolk, Va., and San Diego, Calif. In these communities, CAQH member plans and local health organizations are supplying area health care providers, educators and employers with tools to educate consumers about using antibiotics wisely. More information can be found at http://www.caqh.org/antibioticsinfo.

## Literacy and Understanding Prescription Drug Labels

| Level of Literacy | Percent That Could Read Label Accurately | Percent That Could Demonstrate Correct Number of Pills to Be Taken |
|---|---|---|
| Adequate | 89.4% | 80.2% |
| Marginal | 84.1% | 62.8% |
| Low | 70.7% | 34.7% |

*American Academy of Family Physicians,*
*"Study Finds Many Patients Misunderstand*
*Prescription Drug Labels," December 6, 2006. www.aafp.org.*

"Antibiotic resistance is a much more significant problem than most people realize," said Robert Scalettar, M.D., CAQH chair, SAS initiative, and corporate medical director, Anthem Blue Cross and Blue Shield. "With many serious bacterial infections in the United States and abroad developing resistance, it's crucial that we take action now."

## Confused, Yet Concerned

Despite these findings, consumers do take the consequences of antibiotic resistance seriously. According to the survey, just as many Americans (70 percent) are concerned about antibiotic resistance as West Nile Virus, compared to anthrax (53 percent) and smallpox (49 percent).

## Not What the Doctor Ordered

The survey indicates a great deal of misinformation among consumers concerning the appropriate use of antibiotics. One-third of Americans have taken their health into their own hands and stopped taking an antibiotic before finishing the prescribed amount. Of those who did not finish their medication, 64 percent said they stopped taking it because they were feeling better, and 44 percent said they save the leftover medication for the next time they are ill. Not finishing a course of antibiotics or using leftovers for subsequent illnesses means Americans are not getting the full dosage needed to completely kill a bacterial infection.

## Antibiotics in the Home

Antibiotic use is prevalent amongst Americans. Nearly all have used antibiotics (96 percent), and one-quarter currently have antibiotics in their households. Of those with antibiotics at home, 39 percent of these individuals say the medicine is from a previous prescription, while 36 percent say someone in the household is currently using them.

## About CAQH and the Survey

The Council for Affordable Quality Healthcare (CAQH) is a not-for-profit alliance of America's leading health plans and networks committed to improving the quality of health care and reducing administrative burdens for patients, physicians and payers. Created in 1999, CAQH member organizations provide health care coverage for more than 100 million Americans. CAQH created the Save Antibiotic Strength campaign in partnership with the Centers for Disease Control and Prevention (CDC), the Alliance for the Prudent Use of Antibiotics (APUA), and other leading community and health care organizations across the country to provide Americans with the information they need to use antibiotics wisely.

As part of its Save Antibiotic Strength initiative, CAQH commissioned a national survey to understand how Americans view and use prescription antibiotics. The survey, conducted by Harris Interactive between Oct. 10, 2002 to Oct. 13, 2002, polled a representative sample of 1,000 adults ages 18 and older [and] has a margin of error of plus or minus 3.1

percent. In most of the questions, the respondents had the opportunity to select more than one statement, or none of the statements.

VIEWPOINT *2*

> *"Reasons cited by doctors for overprescribing antibiotics include diagnostic uncertainty, time pressure on physicians, and patient demand."*

# Doctors Overprescribe Antibiotics for Many Reasons

### U.S. Food and Drug Administration

*The U.S. Food and Drug Administration (FDA) holds the responsibility of protecting the public health by assuring the efficacy, security, and safety of drugs, medical devices, cosmetics, the nation's food supply, and so on. In the following viewpoint, the FDA contends that the nation is facing an antibiotic resistance problem. The reason for the developing antibiotic resistance comes mainly from physicians overprescribing medications. Doctors cite time pressure and patient demand as some reasons why they overprescribe antibiotics.*

As you read, consider the following questions:

1. The prescription of antibiotics in an outpatient setting can be reduced by what percentage according to the CDC?

2. What are three main reasons doctors give for overprescribing antibiotics?

U.S. Food and Drug Administration, "Battle of the Bugs: Fighting Antibiotic Resistance," fda.gov, May 1, 2009. Reproduced by permission.

3. What common illnesses do not benefit from antibiotics according to the article?

In 1999, 10 federal agencies and departments, led by the Department of Health & Human Services, formed a task force to tackle the problem of antimicrobial resistance. Co-chaired by the CDC [Centers for Disease Control and Prevention], the FDA [U.S. Food and Drug Administration], and the National Institutes of Health, the task force issued a plan of action in 2001. Task force agencies continue to accomplish the activities set forth in the plan. The success of the plan—known as the Public Health Action Plan to Combat Antimicrobial Resistance—depends on the cooperation of many entities, such as state and local health agencies, universities, professional societies, pharmaceutical companies, health care professionals, agricultural producers, and the public.

All of these groups must work together if the antibiotic resistance problem is to be remedied, says Mark Goldberger, M.D., director of the FDA office responsible for reviewing antibiotic drugs. "This is a very serious problem. We need to do two things: facilitate the development of new antimicrobial therapy while at the same time preserve the usefulness of current and new drugs."

## Preserving Antibiotics' Usefulness

Two main types of germs—bacteria and viruses—cause most infections, according to the CDC. But while antibiotics can kill bacteria, they do not work against viruses—and it is viruses that cause colds, the flu, and most sore throats. In fact, only 15 percent of sore throats are caused by the bacterium *Streptococcus pyogenes*, which results in strep throat. In addition, viruses cause most sinus infections, coughs, and bronchitis. And fluid in the middle ear, a common occurrence in children, does not usually warrant treatment with antibiotics unless there are other symptoms.

## MRSA Defined

MRSA infection is caused by *Staphylococcus aureus* bacteria—often called "staph." MRSA stands for methicillin-resistant *Staphylococcus aureus*. It's a strain of staph that's resistant to the broad-spectrum antibiotics commonly used to treat it. MRSA can be fatal.

Most MRSA infections occur in hospitals or other health care settings, such as nursing homes and dialysis centers. It's known as health care–associated MRSA, or HA-MRSA. Older adults and people with weakened immune systems are at most risk of HA-MRSA.

*Mayo Clinic Staff, "MRSA Infection,"*
*MayoClinic.com, May 30, 2008.*

Nevertheless, "Every year, tens of millions of prescriptions for antibiotics are written to treat viral illnesses for which these antibiotics offer no benefits," says David Bell, M.D., the CDC's antimicrobial resistance coordinator. According to the CDC, antibiotic prescribing in outpatient settings could be reduced by more than 30 percent without adversely affecting patient health.

Reasons cited by doctors for overprescribing antibiotics include diagnostic uncertainty, time pressure on physicians, and patient demand. Physicians are pressured by patients to prescribe antibiotics, says Bell. "People don't want to miss work, or they have a sick child who kept the whole family up all night, and they're willing to try anything that might work." It may be easier for the physician pressed for time to write a prescription for an antibiotic than it is to explain why it might be better not to use one.

But by taking an antibiotic, a person may be doubly harmed, according to Bell. First, it offers no benefit for viral infections, and second, it increases the chance of a drug-resistant infection appearing at a later time.

"Antibiotic resistance is not just a problem for doctors and scientists," says Bell. "Everybody needs to help deal with this. An important way that people can help directly is to understand that common illnesses like colds and the flu do not benefit from antibiotics and to not request them to treat these illnesses." . . .

Another concern to some health experts is the escalating use of antibacterial soaps, detergents, lotions, and other household items. "There has never been evidence that they have a public health benefit," says [Stuart] Levy [a physician and president of the Alliance for the Prudent Use of Antibiotics]. "Good soap and water is sufficient in most cases." Antibacterial products should be reserved for the hospital setting, for sick people coming home from the hospital, and for those with compromised immune systems, says Levy.

To decrease both demand and overprescribing, the FDA and the CDC have launched antibiotic resistance campaigns aimed at health care professionals and the public. A nationwide ad campaign developed by the FDA's Center for Drug Evaluation and Research emphasizes to health care professionals the prudent use of antibiotics and offers them an educational brochure to distribute to patients.

The FDA published a final rule in February 2003 that requires specific language on human antibiotic labels to encourage doctors to prescribe them only when truly necessary. The rule also requires a statement in the labeling encouraging doctors to counsel their patients about the proper use of these drugs.

> *"Spend an extra five minutes talking to your patients about their medical problems, and you can send them away happy and without unnecessary medicine."*

# Doctors Overprescribe Antibiotics Because of Patient Expectations

*Zachary Meisel*

*Zachary Meisel is a practicing emergency physician and a Robert Wood Johnson Foundation clinical scholar at the University of Pennsylvania. In the following viewpoint, he argues that doctors often prescribe antibiotics based on patient expectations rather than solely on medical necessity. Meisel also notes that doctors may prescribe antibiotics in emergency room situations in which they cannot rely upon patients to pursue follow-up care if a condition worsens. Meisel concludes that individual patient care will often trump public health concerns about the dangers of over-prescribing antibiotics and creating drug-resistant bacterial strains.*

As you read, consider the following questions:

1. What did the mother Meisel saw in the ER specifically want for her daughter?

2. According to researchers, which patients were most satisfied with their care when they left the ER?

3. Did Meisel prescribe antibiotics to the mother who wanted them, and was the mother happy with his decision?

While working a busy night shift in the ER [emergency room] recently, I evaluated a 13-month-old girl. On her chart, the triage nurse had written: "Infant with fever and runny nose. Mother here for antibiotics." The baby was fussy but probably more tired than uncomfortable. Between her squirms, she cooed and smiled at me. Her anxious and upset mother, however, was in far worse shape, repeatedly sticking a rubber bulb syringe up her infant's nostrils in a futile attempt to suck out an endless stream of snot. The mom was also really mad: She had been waiting for more than three hours for a doctor to see her daughter. Now she wanted antibiotics: specifically, a prescription for bubble-gum-flavored amoxicillin.

## Parents Want Antibiotics

By my assessment, the child was not acutely ill: She'd had a low-grade fever for two days, her mother said, and a mild cough, but she had clear lungs and appeared well-hydrated. Her eardrum may have had some fluid behind it but wasn't red or bulging. Just as the baby was trying to put my stethoscope in her mouth, paramedics pushed through the ambulance doors with a patient who was having an acute stroke. I had to decide right then if I was going to give this mother the antibiotics she wanted, even though I thought her daughter probably didn't need them.

The profligate prescription of antibiotics—for children and adults with upper respiratory infections, sinus infections, and even middle-ear infections—is a problem because most of these illnesses are caused by viruses, not bacteria, which are what conventional antibiotics attack. Of more concern is the direct connection between antibiotic use and the emergence of drug-resistant "superbugs": As the medicine eliminates germs that are sensitive to it, drug-resistant mutant strains prosper. The result is a major public-health problem. Antibiotic-resistant infections such as methicillin-resistant *Staphylococcus aureus* [or MRSA] may cause more deaths in the United States than AIDS does.

## Virus or Bacteria?

In the doctor's office or the ER, it's hard to tell the difference between bacterial and viral infections, and so doctors are tempted to prescribe antibiotics whenever they're unsure. That's especially true when doctors think that patients expect to take the medicine home, according to a recent study. Investigators interviewed patients with respiratory infections who went to the ER in 10 hospitals affiliated with medical schools, asking whether the patients expected to receive antibiotics and about whether they were satisfied with the care they received when they were discharged. The researchers also asked physicians why they prescribed antibiotics. The main conclusion was that doctors were significantly more likely to prescribe if they believed that patients expected them to—but did a lousy job predicting which patients those actually were. And the patients most satisfied with their care were the ones who left the ER with a better understanding of their condition, antibiotics or no antibiotics. The take-home message for doctors like me: Spend an extra five minutes talking to your patients about their medical problems, and you can send them away happy and without unnecessary medicine.

So once doctors absorb the result of this study and similar investigations, will they write fewer prescriptions? I bet not. To give out fewer antibiotics, the doctors will have to believe that their patients won't benefit from them. If you look closely at the ER study, 73 percent of the patients who received antibiotics for acute bronchitis had illnesses that were either deemed by their doctors to have likely been caused by a bacteria or to have origins that were in that gray toss-up area between a bacteria and a virus. If the doctors were right, and these were bacterial infections, they would, in fact, warrant antibiotics. Also, in many of these cases, the doctors gave other persuasive reasons for choosing antibiotics, including "ill appearance of the patient" and "concern about follow-up."

## Follow-Up Is Difficult

In my ER world, these factors, if intangible, are understood to be really important in helping us decide how to treat patients. The real dilemma of antibiotic prescriptions is that the most serious consequence for writing them unnecessarily is not a risk to the individual patient but the emergence of the super-bugs that pose a risk to public health in general.

Nowhere is this tension between individual care and public health greater than in the ER. Office-based cultures [tests] for bacterial infections, which take days to turn around, are not feasible in what we call "the trenches." And because follow-up can never be assured, it's hard to follow recommendations such as those of the American Academy of Pediatrics, which advocates "watch and wait" for 48 to 72 hours for children with middle-ear infections rather than an immediate dose of antibiotics. If we overprescribe antibiotics in the ER, that's because in the trenches the care of one patient often trumps the care of the public. Maybe that's myopic, but there you have it. And it is why efforts to reduce antibiotic use by giving out more information about resistant infections or teaching doctors how to manage patient expectations may ultimately fall flat.

In the end, I did not prescribe antibiotics for the 13-month-old baby. Instead, I took the time to explain thoroughly why I didn't think she needed them (while my colleague took care of the stroke patient). But no matter what that study says, that mother left in a huff—highly dissatisfied, I can assure you. I'm not sure what I'll do the next time I see a similar case. Perhaps I will refuse to write the prescription again, notching another victory for public health. But, for all I know, something intangible will be different: Perhaps the kid just won't look right, or maybe the mother or father will seem too disorganized to be relied on to return if the kid worsens. And that may persuade me to send them home with a bottle of pink-bubble-gum-flavored amoxicillin. It's likely that the fussy kid and his parents won't sleep any better that night. But I will.

> "I think what has happened is that frequently inadequate prescribing of antibiotics over the past 50 years . . . was leaving a residue of 'stunned' but not killed bugs in patients, which over a long period developed a degree of resistance to antibiotics."

# Doctors Are Underprescribing Antibiotics

*Ron Graves*

*Ron Graves is a British survivor of myalgic encephalomyelitis (ME), a poorly understood condition characterized by chronic exhaustion and chronic obstructive pulmonary disease (COPD), a long-standing lung ailment. In the following viewpoint, he argues that the difficulty in getting doctors to prescribe large doses of antibiotics has made it hard for him to control his lung infections. He adds that by underprescribing antibiotics, doctors may fail to kill infections, allowing bacteria to develop resistances. Graves concludes that more research needs to be done into the dangers of underprescribing antibiotics.*

Ron Graves, "MRSA and Antibiotics—An Opinion," Ron's Rants, March 30, 2010. Reproduced by permission of the author.

As you read, consider the following questions:

1. Under what circumstances does Graves say he would always develop an infection?

2. What does Graves say he had to do in the 2000s to get antibiotic treatment?

3. According to Graves, how often has he taken 500 mg Amoxyl since he began importing it in 2004?

We are routinely told that one of the reasons for the rise of antibiotic-resistant infections like MRSA [methicillin-resistant *Staphylococcus aureus*, a dangerous drug-resistant strain of bacteria], in hospitals, is the over-prescribing of antibiotics. As someone whose life has depended on antibiotics (I have Stage 4 COPD), for as long as they've been available to the public (which is longer than most people realise—they date from about 1953, when penicillin became widely available—prior to that, and afterwards too, as it was cheaper, the sulphonamide drug M&B [sulfapyridine] kept me alive), I'm not convinced.

## Reduced Antibiotics Will Not Stop Infections

Whenever I've been admitted to hospital—or even when I've hung around outpatients for too long (time was when an OPD [outpatient department] visit would tie up half a day, easily)—I've always come away with an infection I didn't go in with—they've always been there in some form. It would be surprising if they were not, given that the average patient has very little concept of hygiene.

In my case, it would normally be a respiratory infection (my weak spot), though on one occasion, almost 50 years ago, it was a tissue-consuming post-operative bug that took months of daily, and painful, treatment to clear up. A matter of scraping off the necrotic tissue and soaking the raw wound in a strong sterilising solution—about as much fun as it sounds—

before applying an antibiotic dressing. Looking back, I can't understand why systemic antibiotics weren't used to supplement the topical application. MRSA-like pathogens certainly aren't as new in a hospital environment as NICE [National Institute of Health and Clinical Excellence] would like us to believe.

Throughout the eighties [1980s], I had doctors who had no worries about providing me with stocks of antibiotics to take at my discretion—it reduced their workload and meant I could treat infections as soon as they appeared. It was a system that worked very well, but came to an end in the early nineties [1990s] when one of them moved on, and the other retired. It was clear, though, that I was in a minority, and most of my peers didn't get this treatment.

I began to notice, in the early '90s, when I had to attend the surgery every few weeks with a spate of respiratory infections, that the quantities of antibiotics prescribed had been drastically reduced—never any more than 7 days' worth, and at the lowest available strength, and 3 a day instead of 4 (not GP [general practitioner] parsimony, but in the advice in the British National Formulary—the GP's drug bible—how much influence NICE has on that advice, I don't know, but I suspect a lot).

For me and, I suspect, for most people with a cycle of chronic respiratory infection and re-infection, this proved inadequate. True, it would knock back the infection but, after a few weeks it would rally and reappear, and I'd be back at the doctor's again.

Some years earlier, in 1980, and again in 1981, I had two long bouts of infection (three months+), that refused to go away. During both events I was treated with small quantities of antibiotics, and had to re-attend the surgery every week or two for a new prescription of a different antibiotic. Eventually, erythromycin did the trick, but I'm pretty sure any of its pre-decessors would have done so at a high enough dose, for long enough.

I believe that had I been treated then—as I was in the *late* eighties, by a different doctor—with *massive* doses of drugs (for example, then I had a stock of 3-gram sachets of Amoxyl [an antibiotic], taken 3 times a day—hugely effective), my re-covery would have been much faster in both cases, and I think I would have been able to continue working for longer. I also believe that I was left with a legacy of bacteria that were resis-tant, to a degree, to many of the antibiotics I'd taken.

## More Antibiotics Are Needed

It's quite clear from those two experiences, that *under*-prescribing is a very real problem and has been for a long time, with no reason to assume it's not common.

In the early 2000s, antibiotic prescribing took a turn for the worse, and it became almost impossible, for me at least, to get treatment without submitting a sputum sample for labora-tory analysis. In theory this should have taken 24 hours; in practise it often took a week. Aside from meaning I spent a week getting worse, it meant I had to make yet another trip to the doctor to get my prescription which, all too often, was for a drug that I knew would disagree violently with me—for some reason the lab's recommendation was always for a very new drug—quite possibly the one the last drug company rep had been pushing—and not for more established drugs that I knew would get the job done without harming me in the pro-cess.

It reached a farcical peak when, having had the usual week's worth of meds, which hadn't worked, I went back for more, only to be told I would have to submit to *another* spu-tum test! It was at that point I realised that the health of the patient has ceased to matter, and stupidity and cant had taken over—we were, effectively, carrying the can for all the alleged over-prescribing. I believe now as I believed then that this is a crock, and used by NICE as a lever to cut down antibiotic prescribing.

As an aside, in my experience, older doctors are more likely to prescribe more generously than youngsters, and ignore NICE's whinging [whining]. A state of affairs which won't be allowed to continue. http://ronsrants.wordpress.com/2008/12/10/nice-rules-literally/.

In 2004, realising that I could legally import drugs for my own use, I started buying my own supplies of 500 mg Amoxyl caps. This meant I could tackle an infection as soon as it reared its ugly head, before it had time to make me ill (trust me, if you've lived with respiratory infections your whole life, you learn to recognise the signs of an incipient crisis several days before it actually makes you ill, or it would be apparent to a GP). I take one every eight hours when needed (very occasionally two)—not just for a week, but for as long as it takes. In the last four years, I've only needed to see my GP once, with a bug that wasn't susceptible to Amoxyl, so the facts speak for themselves.

Or, if I catch it early, just for a few days, though I'm currently recovering from pneumonia, and getting to the end of a three-week course. A few days or several weeks—the bottom line is I can take them for as long as proves necessary, with zero hassle. And I've only needed a doctor 3 or 4 times in 7 years (and one of those was for flu), so I'm doing something right.

To sum up, I think what has happened is that frequently inadequate prescribing of antibiotics over the past 50 years, coupled with patient ignorance about finishing the course (you don't stop just because you start to feel better!), was leaving a residue of "stunned" but not killed bugs in patients, which over a long period developed a degree of resistance to antibiotics—a resistance that was passed on to each successive generation, and built up substantial reservoirs of antibiotic-resistant bacteria in the UK [United Kingdom] population. If this was happening with me, how many thousands of other people were having the same experience? Multiply my experience by that of everybody with probably any form of infection, and *under-prescribing* may well be the real culprit, not the alleged over-prescribing that has blighted the lives of so many of us who depend on antibiotics for our very lives.

> *"A doctor is an expert in knowing which antibiotic to use for specific ailments. If an untrained person uses the wrong antibiotic his condition may get worse and he may wind up in the hospital."*

# Buying Antibiotics Without a Prescription Is Dangerous

*Corey Nahman*

*Corey Nahman is a registered pharmacist in the state of New York and publishes the Web site InternetDrugNews.com. In the following viewpoint, Nahman reports that he and investigators were able to easily purchase antibiotics without a prescription from pet stores, ethnic groceries, and other locations. He argues that this is dangerous, since patients do not have the knowledge to use antibiotics safely. Nahman concludes that patients should not take antibiotics without a prescription but suggests that they will probably continue to do so as long as obtaining antibiotics is so easy.*

As you read, consider the following questions:

1. If you walk into a pet store, what two things does Nahman say you may be surprised to learn?
2. What are three reasons Nahman gives that people may try to obtain antibiotics without getting a prescription?
3. According to Nahman, what drug/food interaction can cause fatal heart arrhythmias?

W e wanted to determine if it was possible to obtain antibiotics without a prescription and how people do it.

In the United States, there are 4 ways to obtain antibiotics without a prescription: buy them in a pet store, drive down to Mexico, buy them in an ethnic market/convenience store or buy them on the Internet.

## Pet Stores and the Internet

Here is a loophole I learned about when I began training as a pharmacist thirty years ago. If you walk into [the] aquarium section of any well-stocked pet store, you may be surprised to learn 2 things:

(A) Fish diseases are treated with human antibiotics.

(B) You don't need a prescription to purchase antibiotics for fish.

We visited 6 pet stores in the New York City area—2 national chains, a regional chain and 3 independently owned pet shops.

Both national chain pet stores we visited had antibiotics for sale. Most of the formulations were available as liquid gel drops or powders that are difficult for people to take. However, we were able to obtain tablets of triple sulfa (a cocktail of 3 broad-spectrum [usable against many infections] sulfa antibiotics) and tetracycline tablets on the Web sites of these chains.

The regional chain pet store and all three mom-and-pop pet stores sold tetracycline, erythromycin and ampicillin in tablet and capsule form.

On the Internet, it was easy to find amoxicillin, ampicillin, tetracycline, cephalexin, metronidazole and erythromycin for sale without a prescription by searching Google for the term "fish antibiotics."

It is a bad idea for people to take veterinary medicines, but chemically the drugs are the same as what you find in a human pharmacy.

According to anecdotal reports, the fact that one can obtain antibiotics in this manner is common knowledge among branches of the armed forces.

Importing nonprescription antibiotics over the Internet into the United States is a low priority for the authorities compared to narcotics and controlled substances. When was the last time you read about someone being arrested for importing Cipro [brand name of antibiotic ciprofloxacin] or Augmentin [brand name of antibiotic amoxicillin and clavulanic acid] into the USA?

Here's how it works: As long as the pharmacy is located in a country that does not require a doctor's prescription for a drug, they are happy to sell you whatever you need (other than controlled substances) without a prescription. You might be bending the law, but the authorities look the other way. . . .

## Ethnic Groceries and Mexico

Many ethnic grocery/convenience stores such as bodegas (small grocery/convenience stores found in Latino neighborhoods), sell antibiotics.

Since I live in New York City, we conducted our experiment in Washington Heights, a vibrant immigrant community with a large Spanish-speaking population.

## Antibiotics in Latino Communities

Antibiotic self-medication [by Latinos in the United States] may not be affected by greater access to care because of the belief that physician consultation is not necessary before treatment. Using such strategies as acquiring antibiotics without a prescription from *tiendas* [Latino groceries] and pharmacies within the United States does seem to be a cultural artifact of the loosely regulated sale of antibiotics in Latin America. . . .

Our findings highlight the need to devise effective interventions to deal with self-medication with antibiotics in the Latino community. Education alone may not be enough. Data from New York City indicated that in Latino neighborhoods, as opposed to predominantly non-Hispanic black or non-Hispanic white neighborhoods, antibiotics . . . were remarkably available in the neighborhood stores. . . . It may be that a greater focus on regulation of the selling of antibiotics . . . is necessary.

*Arch G. Mainous III, Vanessa A. Diaz, and Mark Carnemolla,*
*"A Community Intervention to Decrease Antibiotics Used for*
*Self-Medication Among Latino Adults,"*
Annals of Family Medicine, *vol. 7, no. 6,*
*November/December 2009.*

Our undercover investigator (a middle-aged woman) went into several bodegas and explained that she had a sore throat and needed antibiotics. Two out of seven stores had antibiotics for sale.

One store had "Gimalxina," a brand name for amoxicillin. She bought 20 capsules for $10.00. Another store had generic ampicillin and tetracycline for $0.60 per pill. They also had other medicines for sale (such as diuretics [drugs that increase urination] and birth control pills, but that's another story).

People who buy medicine from ethnic markets are usually poor and originate from cultures where buying antibiotics over the counter is the norm.

A 2002 *New York Times* article indicated that Chinese and Russian immigrants easily purchase antibiotics and other prescription drugs in small markets.

Selling prescription medicines to Americans is a huge industry in Mexico. The main shopping streets in border towns such as Tijuana and Nogales are lined with pharmacies.

We took a bus from downtown San Diego across the border to Tijuana, Mexico. There, we were able to buy 14 tablets of brand-name Cipro 500 mg [milligrams] (ciprofloxacin) for $35.00 US. 96 capsules of amoxicillin 500 mg went for $18.95. Levaquin [antibiotic] was harder to find, but we were able to buy 15 tablets of the generic for about $25.00.

South of the border you can walk into any drugstore and buy antibiotics over the counter. It's just like buying Tylenol or Advil [over-the-counter pain relievers]. No prescriptions are needed and nobody asks any questions. So, if you live within driving distance of the Mexican border (like in San Diego or El Paso) this is a piece of cake.

## Why People Get Nonprescription Antibiotics

Why not do what everyone else does—go to the doctor, get a prescription and take it to the drugstore?

There are many reasons people don't want to obtain antibiotics the traditional way:

- *Persistent Infections*—such as urinary tract infections. You feel burning discomfort down there with an urgency to urinate and you know right away what you have because you get it all the time. It is a pain in the neck having to run to the doctor for an expensive examination when you know what you have and what you need.

- *Skin Conditions*—people who suffer from acne or rosacea [a common skin condition] often take antibiotics prophylactically to prevent flare-ups. They prefer to buy a large quantity of medicine for a cheap price rather than visiting [a] dermatologist every time they need a refill.

- *Poverty, Lack of Insurance, Cultural Norms*—many people (such as undocumented immigrants) work for small businesses. They get zero benefits. They can't afford the doctor and they can't afford American drug prices. Often, they come from cultures where prescriptions are not required for antibiotics.

## Nonprescription Antibiotics Are Dangerous

If you get your antibiotics without going to a doctor and getting a prescription, you can get yourself in trouble:

- Misdiagnosis

Antibiotics are not a cure-all. They are only effective against bacterial illnesses. They are not effective against viral illnesses.

Antibiotics are designed to combat specific ailments. For instance, penicillins (a family of drugs with names ending in "-cillin" such as peni*cillin*, amoxi*cillin*, ampi*cillin*) are effective against streptococcal infections, syphilis, and Lyme disease, but for community-acquired pneumonia, bacterial diarrhea, mycoplasmal infections or gonorrhea you would be better off using a quinolone (a family of drugs with names ending in "-oxacin" such as levoflo*xacin* (Levaquin) or ciproflo*xacin* (Cipro).

A doctor is an expert in knowing which antibiotic to use for specific ailments. If an untrained person uses the wrong antibiotic his condition may get worse and he may wind up in the hospital.

• Side Effects

Antibiotics can cause side effects. If you take an antibiotic that you are allergic to you could develop an anaphylactic [severe allergic] reaction, go into shock and die. Other antibiotic side effects include nausea and diarrhea, abdominal pain, liver toxicity, brain and kidney damage or even pseudomembranous colitis [a potentially life-threatening infection of the colon].

• Interactions (Drug, Food, Alcohol)

Certain antibiotics should not be mixed with other drugs, foods or alcohol. Mixing cephlosporins (such as cephalexin) with alcohol could cause nausea or abdominal cramps. Drinking grapefruit juice with erythromycins or taking erythromycin with theophylline (a drug used for respiratory ailments) can cause fatal heart arrhythmias [abnormal electrical activity in the heart]. There are many other interactions that doctors know about but you don't.

• Resistance

No-prescription antibiotics are likely to be misused leading to drug resistance. Drug-resistant germs are difficult to treat and have spread into the community wreaking havoc on our health care institutions.

Buying antibiotics without a doctor's prescription is easy. The drugs are inexpensive. This is a potentially dangerous practice but it is unlikely to stop because it is a low priority for law enforcement institutions.

> *"If you have something that can be detected with a urine test and treated with a course of antibiotics then there's no reason why this has to be dealt with in a clinical setting."*

# Making Antibiotics Available Without a Prescription for Some Conditions Can Improve Care

*Petra Boynton*

*Petra Boynton is a lecturer in International Health Services Research at a London university, where she teaches doctors, nurses, and other health professionals at the postgraduate level. In the following viewpoint, she argues that the British newspaper the* Daily Mail *is a scaremonger when it suggests that over-the-counter testing and antibiotic treatment for the sexually transmitted disease chlamydia will increase promiscuity. Boynton notes that testing/treatment for chlamydia is already easily available through clinics in Britain. She says that making it available through pharmacies will take a burden off the health care system and give individuals greater control over their sexual health.*

Petra Boynton, "Over the Counter Tests for Chlamydia—An Old Story That Counts as 'News' in the *Daily Mail*," drpetra.co.uk, August 26, 2008. Reproduced by permission.

As you read, consider the following questions:

1. How many people in the United Kingdom under the age of twenty-five are affected by chlamydia, according to Boynton?

2. Why does Boynton say that sixteen-year-olds probably will not be using the test/treatment package?

3. Why does Boynton say that it is not a good idea to test people with chlamydia for other sexually transmitted infections?

We're all familiar with the *Daily Mail*'s take on health stories. They're super keen on promoting quackery, bad science and misunderstanding evidence. . . .

## Moralizing About Chlamydia

Today there's another great example of bad health reporting from the *Mail* with their so-called exposé on over the counter chlamydia [a sexually transmitted bacterial infection] testing and treatment. In the piece the *Mail* describes over the counter testing/treatment as not only a new phenomenon, but one that will 'increase promiscuity'.

It fits with their usual agenda of sex negative coverage and moralising about relationships. They have a track record of opposing everything from promoting homosexuality to providing school sex education. Today they're opposing people managing their own sexual health.

Let's look at the evidence that the *Daily Mail* decided to ignore.

Chlamydia is a highly prevalent infection in the UK [United Kingdom] with 1 in 10 people aged under 25 affected. It is often symptomless and can lead to problems with infertility in later life if left untreated. It is also easily prevented by condom use and can be diagnosed with a simple urine test and treated effectively with antibiotics.

So although it is very common, it is easily preventable and easily treated.

Currently if you think you may have chlamydia (or any sexually transmitted infection) you can get tested (and treated if needed) at your GU clinic [genitourinary clinic, which treats genital diseases] or some GP [general practitioner] surgeries. Testing and treatment is free although there may be a waiting list to get treated and to receive results of tests.

Our sexual health services are overstretched, and current thinking in sexual health care suggests that for many infections people can 'self manage'. Meaning if you have something that can be detected with a urine test and treated with a course of antibiotics then there's no reason why this has to be dealt with in a clinical setting. It can be managed within a community setting.

Which is where the pharmacy comes in. There have been numerous trials of delivering testing and treatment schemes for chlamydia via pharmacy settings which have all shown that it is a feasible means of offering sexual health care. People prefer the intimate setting of the pharmacy and are happy to talk to the pharmacist about their sexual health. As well as being tested and offered treatment where necessary there is also the opportunity to provide additional sexual health advice, condoms and a referral to GU services if it seems necessary.

These schemes have been published in scientific journals and many Primary Care Trusts are now encouraging chlamydia testing and treatment within the community. So the *Daily Mail* story isn't exactly cutting edge news.

Okay, so they're talking about a paid-for service but again these have been available for many years. People can arrange testing and treatment through private clinics or through Web sites. . . .

## No Increase in Promiscuity

The *Mail* story incorrectly suggests that having over the counter testing/treatment will lead to an increase in promiscu-

## Chlamydia in the US

Chlamydia is the most frequently reported sexually transmitted disease (STD) caused by *bacteria* . . . in the US.

An estimated 2.8 million Americans get chlamydia each year. Women are often re-infected . . . if their sex partners are not treated.

Re-infections place women at higher risk for serious reproductive health complications, including infertility. . . .

Because there are often *no* symptoms, people who are infected may unknowingly pass chlamydia to their sex partners.

*Medic8, "Chlamydia." www.medic8.com.*

ity—but we already have an epidemic of STIs [sexually transmitted infections] we need to sort out. Having self-testing/treatment methods available should reduce STIs and make it more likely people will use condoms in [the] future as they'll be brought into contact with services to advise them.

Moreover it wrongly implies that 16-year-olds (and upwards) will be using the test/treatment package. This is nonsensical since it's a paid-for service—and services to test/treat teenagers and young adults already exist for free! It is more likely that older adults will use the paid-for service, but we still need to advertise the availability of free services for testing and treatment.

Finally the *Mail* quotes a practitioner who claims that people with chlamydia should be tested for other STIs. This is a real worry as it indicates the practitioner is not up to date with our knowledge of STIs. We used to believe it was right to test for all STIs routinely. So if someone presented at a clinic with chlamydia we'd test them for everything including syphilis and HIV. The overwhelming evidence showed that most people presenting with symptomless infections like chlamydia only had that infection—so testing for everything was overkill and wasted important staff time and funds.

Having a test over the counter does not prevent someone [from] getting further testing in a clinic if they are worried. But it does mean they get to talk to a practitioner quickly and can be given safer sex advice that could prevent them getting infections in the future.

The *Mail* is simply scaremongering with this feature. They've not read the evidence or understood how sexual health care is developing. We won't get more promiscuous youngsters as a result of having services available over the counter—but having an additional way to get testing/ treatment could remove pressure on overstretched services and allow people to take control over their sexual health—and what can be so wrong with that?

# Periodical Bibliography

*The following articles have been selected to supplement the diverse views presented in this chapter.*

Associated Press          "Mexico Sets Plan to Crack Down on Antibiotic Sales," *Brownsville Herald*, March 26, 2010. www.brownsvilleherald.com.

BBC News                  "Chlamydia Drug Over-the-Counter," August 5, 2008. http://news.bbc.co.uk.

Kathleen Blanchard        "Lawsuit Fears Potential Cause of Increase in MRSA Rates," eMaxHealth.com, December 21, 2009. www.emaxhealth.com.

Donna Haupt               "Overprescription of Antibiotics," FamilyEducation, n.d. www.familyeducation.com.

Jenny Hope                "Over-the-Counter Chlamydia Kit 'Will Boost Promiscuity', Warn Experts," *Daily Mail*, August 6, 2008. www.dailymail.co.uk.

Arch G. Mainous III,      "A Community Intervention to Decrease Antibiotics Used for Self-Medication Among Latino Adults," *Annals of Family Medicine*, vol. 7, no. 6, November/December 2009. www.annfammed .org.
Vanessa A. Diaz, and
Mark Carnemolla

Mayo Clinic Staff         "Antibiotics: Misuse Puts You and Others at Risk," MayoClinic.com, February 6, 2010. www .mayoclinic.com.

Medical News Today        "What Are Antibiotics? How Do Antibiotics Work?" April 20, 2009. www.medicalnewstoday .com.

Science*Daily*            "Changing the Way Antibiotics Are Prescribed May Be Key to Controlling Epidemics," February 22, 2008. www.sciencedaily.com.

Jan Velinger              "Awareness Campaign Takes Aim at Doctors' Over-Prescription of Antibiotics," Radio Prague, November 19, 2008. www.radio.cz/en.

# CHAPTER 2

# How Should Antibiotics Be Used in Agriculture?

# Chapter Preface

In factory farming, antibiotics are used intensively to prevent infection in animals living in extremely close quarters. Antibiotics are also used in low doses "as growth promoters that increase the animal's output and value," according to the State Environmental Resource Center.

The regular use of antibiotics in agriculture may, over time, cause the development of antibiotic-resistant bacteria. One particularly worrisome possibility is the development of resistant strains of *Salmonella*. According to a September 20, 2006, fact sheet by the U.S. Department of Agriculture (USDA), *Salmonella* is "the most frequently reported cause of foodborne illness." *Salmonella* bacteria are found in the guts of many animals, including chickens. Humans are usually infected when they eat eggs or poultry that have been in contact with animal feces and have not been sufficiently cooked.

Symptoms of salmonellosis include diarrhea, cramps, and fever, as well as chills, nausea, and vomiting. Most people recover without treatment within four to seven days. According to the USDA fact sheet, however, infections "can be life-threatening especially for infants and young children, pregnant women and their unborn babies, and older adults," as well as those weakened by other illnesses.

Many link the development of *Salmonella* bacteria that are resistant to antibiotics to the use of antibiotics in agriculture. For example, Dale Keiger reports in a June 2009 article in *John Hopkins* magazine that some medical professionals connect resistant *Salmonella* to the fact that "factory chicken farms routinely feed antibiotics to their flocks, to accelerate growth, and the drugs generate resistance." In an April 2005 fact sheet on its Web site, the World Health Organization (WHO) agrees, noting that antibiotic-resistant *Salmonella* bacteria seem to have developed after the main antibiotics used to combat *Sal-*

*monella* started to be included in animal feed. The WHO adds, "Multidrug-resistant (MDR) strains of *Salmonella* are now encountered frequently and the rates of multidrug-resistance have increased considerably in recent years."

The WHO points to two main dangers in regards to drug-resistant *Salmonella*. The first is that some people may be infected with *Salmonella* who otherwise would not have been. When people receive antibiotics, it affects microbes in their intestinal tract and makes the individuals more vulnerable to infection from antibiotic-resistant bacteria. The WHO estimates that *Salmonella* resistance may result in thirty thousand more *Salmonella* infections and ten more deaths each year in the United States. The other danger is that it will be more difficult to treat those who are infected. According to the WHO, "persons with infections caused by antimicrobial-resistant *Salmonella* have been found to be more likely to have bloodstream infection or die within 90 days." To protect against multidrug-resistant *Salmonella*, the WHO recommends a reduction in the use of antibiotics in agriculture and a greater attention to food sanitation.

The viewpoints in this chapter focus on other issues involved in and approaches to the uses of antibiotics in agriculture.

> "Administered at low, subtherapeutic levels, these antibiotics promote the growth and health of animals and the abundance, affordability and safety of dairy, meat and poultry products."

# Antibiotic Use in Animal Agriculture Is Safe and Necessary

*Rod Smith*

*Rod Smith writes regularly for* Feedstuffs, *a weekly newspaper for agribusiness, and its affiliated Web site, Feedstuffs FoodLink. In the following viewpoint, he argues that low-level antibiotic use on farms keeps animals healthy by reducing the risk of infection. He maintains that the reduction of antibiotic use in Europe has resulted in an increase in dangerous infections. He adds that bacterial resistance in humans comes mostly from doctors over-prescribing antibiotics, not from the use of antibiotics on farms.*

As you read, consider the following questions:

1. What does Smith say that researchers at Iowa State University found about the use of antibiotics in pigs?

Rod Smith, "Antibiotics Called Vital, Safe," Feedstuffs FoodLink, August 21, 2009. Copyright © 2009 Feedstuffs FoodLink. Reproduced by permission.

2. According to Smith, why do livestock and poultry producers have no incentive to overuse antibiotics?

3. According to the twenty groups representing livestock producers, what have activist groups long campaigned against?

A merican farmers and ranchers work daily to provide the best management possible for their animals in health and nutrition, housing and handling—practices that include the judicious use of government-approved veterinary medicines such as antibiotics.

## Antibiotics Promote Health

Administered at low, subtherapeutic levels, these antibiotics promote the growth and health of animals and the abundance, affordability and safety of dairy, meat and poultry products.

However, there is opposition to low-level use by interests that believe it is leading to antibiotic resistance in human medicine, a claim for which there is no conclusive practical or scientific evidence. Indeed, there is increasing evidence of just the opposite: The responsible use of antibiotics contributes to improved animal welfare and food safety.

These thoughts were expressed in a letter sent to the White House Aug. 14 [2009] by 20 organizations representing livestock and poultry producers, veterinarians and the grain and feed industries.

The letter was sent to Melody Barnes, domestic policy adviser to President Barack Obama, and to Agriculture Secretary Tom Vilsack and Health & Human Services Secretary Kathleen Sebelius, as well as the Food and Drug Administration [FDA] and the House [of Representatives] and Senate agriculture committees.

The letter contains footnotes documenting scientific studies supporting the groups' position.

The letter refers to two studies released last year:

(1) Researchers at Iowa State University found that pigs not administered antibiotics that got sick had a greater pathogen presence than pigs administered antibiotics that did not get sick.

(2) Researchers at The Ohio State University found that pigs not administered antibiotics that were raised outdoors had more pathogen presence than pigs raised in modern barns and houses with the use of antibiotics.

The letter also refers to an expert report by the Institute of Food Technologists in 2006 concluding that there are "significant human health benefits from subtherapeutic antibiotic use" to reduce *Campylobacter* and *Salmonella* [two kinds of dangerous bacteria] in poultry. The letter notes that the report further states that the elimination of such use would have "little positive effect on resistant bacteria that threaten human health," and in fact, such actions in other countries have, in some cases, led to more antibiotic use to treat sick animals and more resistant bacteria.

The letter says several European nations that banned or restricted the use of certain antimicrobial products are now documenting "a significant increase" in animal diseases—many not seen in Europe in 20 years—and an increase in the use of antibiotics by veterinarians to treat those diseases.

The letter reports research in the Netherlands that found that penicillin and tetracycline resistance in *Salmonella typhimurium* [a bacteria] has increased in people since the implementation of the ban, while the same resistance declined in the U.S. over the same period.

## Evidence Supports Antibiotic Use

Livestock and poultry producers have no incentive to misuse or overuse antibiotics, which are expensive but vital tools for the health and welfare of their animals, according to the letter.

## The Media Sensationalize the Issue of Antibiotics on Farms

News media coverage of the issue [of antibiotics in animal feed] has perpetuated a number of misconceptions ..., chief among them being that farm animals are fed copious amounts of antibiotics from birth to harvest, that livestock veterinarians don't have enough oversight of how antibiotics are used and that producers are not smart enough to use antibiotics responsibly and appropriately.

*Cliff Gauldin, "Antibiotics in Ag Debate Gains Momentum,"*
*Feedstuffs FoodLink, January 18, 2010.*
*www.feedstuffsfoodlink.com.*

Furthermore, the letter notes that the feed and grain industries have feed/food safety and quality assurance programs, and the livestock and poultry industries have programs that train producers in the responsible use of antibiotics, with third-party certification—all developed with advice and recommendations from the American Veterinary Medical Association (AVMA).

Moreover, the letter reports that AVMA last month established an antimicrobial use task force—with representation from several veterinary groups—to conduct two workshops on the issue and has invited representatives to participate from the livestock and poultry sectors, FDA's Center for Veterinary Medicine, the Centers for Disease Control and Prevention and the National Association of State Public Health Veterinarians.

The letter notes that the 20 groups are aware of a letter certain activist groups sent to Barnes last month commending what they believe is the Obama administration's official position on the subtherapeutic use of antibiotics based on FDA Deputy Commissioner Dr. Joshua Sharfstein's testimony to Congress last month.

However, the letter says Sharfstein's testimony referenced only the "idea" of limiting antibiotic use for animals and "stopped far short" of endorsing legislation or presenting the administration's position on the matter.

The letter says the activist groups, which dispatched representatives to testify at the hearing, have long campaigned against "on-farm antibiotic use and other technologies used by farmers, ranchers and veterinarians" to protect animals and keep food safe.

The letter notes that the activist groups offered no new data or information to make their case but, rather, "echoed inaccurate messages" and made no mention of the issue "of overprescription of antibiotics in human medicine or of the increasing data" suggesting that this human exposure to antibiotics "is the greatest factor in acquiring infections with antibiotic-resistant bacteria."

The letter says the activist groups' arguments belie an important lack of understanding about food animal and food production, and their suggestion that shifting the U.S. production system to the European model will eliminate the need for animal health intervention "is naïve." Birds and livestock will be exposed to disease regardless of the production system, the letter notes.

The 20 groups told Barnes they are not—as they are accused of being—"dug in," and they are hoping that there will be a continued discussion "on this complex issue."

Their letter says discussion should offer producers science-based, pragmatic options that are in the best interests of animal health and welfare and provide assurance to the public that antibiotics are vital, effective and safe tools used judiciously and professionally and that do not jeopardize human health.

*"As the bacteria become more resistant to the antibiotics fed to chickens and other animals raised for meat, they may become more resistant to the antibiotics needed to treat sick people."*

# Antibiotic Use in Animal Agriculture Is Dangerous and Unnecessary

*Humane Society of the United States*

*The Humane Society of the United States is an organization that advocates against the mistreatment of animals. In the following viewpoint, the organization argues that antibiotics are used by agribusiness primarily to promote growth in livestock and poultry rather than to prevent disease. The viewpoint argues that widespread use of antibiotics in animal feed has caused the dangerous development of antibiotic resistance in bacteria. The viewpoint also states that, despite industry claims, little financial benefit results from using antibiotics in animal feed. Therefore, the viewpoint concludes, the use of antibiotics in agribusiness should be curtailed.*

Humane Society of the United States, *An HSUS Report: Human Health Implications of Non-Therapeutic Antibiotic Use in Animal Agriculture*, October 20, 2009. Reproduced by permission of The Humane Society of the United States, www.hsus.org.

As you read, consider the following questions:

1. When and where did scientists announce the discovery that antibiotics make chickens grow faster?

2. What evidence does the viewpoint provide that antibiotic-resistant *Campylobacter* is linked to the use of quinolones in chickens?

3. What is the cost in money and lives of antibiotic-resistant infections, according to this viewpoint?

For decades, the U.S. meat industry has fed medically important antibiotics to chickens, pigs, and cows to accelerate their growth and weight gain. A strong scientific consensus exists, asserting that this practice fosters antibiotic resistance in bacteria to the detriment of human health. In response to this public health threat, the European Union has banned the non-therapeutic feeding of antibiotics of human importance to farm animals. Given recent data that suggest an overall lack of financial benefit, the U.S. meat industry has little reason to continue this risky practice.

## Antibiotics and Growth Promotion

At the annual meeting of the American Chemical Society in Philadelphia in 1950, scientists announced the discovery that antibiotics make chickens grow faster. By 1951, the U.S. Food and Drug Administration (FDA) approved the addition of penicillin and tetracycline [both antibiotics] to chicken feed as growth promoters, encouraging pharmaceutical companies to mass-produce antibiotics for animal agriculture. Growing concerns over antibiotic resistance, however, have caused many to reconsider this practice.

Although the European Union has banned the use of antibiotics of human importance in farm animals for non-treatment purposes since 1998, producers in the United States continue to mix more than one dozen different antibiotics into farm animal feed. The Union of Concerned Scientists

(UCS) estimates that 70 percent of antimicrobials used in the United States are fed to chickens, pigs, and cows for non-therapeutic purposes. Additionally, three antibiotics have been approved by the FDA for use in the U.S. aquaculture [fish farming] industry, which consumes more than 50,000 pounds of antibiotics annually. Given the scale and intensification of the poultry industry, however, birds raised for meat have historically swallowed the largest share of antibiotics.

By the 1970s, 100 percent of all commercially raised poultry in the United States were being fed antibiotics. By the late 1990s, poultry producers were using more than 10 million pounds of antibiotics a year, more than a 300-percent increase from the 1980s. These thousands of tons of antibiotics funneled into animal agriculture are not used to treat sick and diseased animals; more than 90 percent of the antibiotics are used to promote weight gain. The majority of the antibiotics produced in the world go not to human medicine but to usage on the farm.

The scientific community is still uncertain as to why the low-level feeding of antibiotics promotes faster weight gain in animals raised for meat. One possible explanation is the "resource allocation theory." Only a certain amount of energy, protein, and other nutrients enter an animal's system at any one time. Resources directed towards mounting an effective immune response are diverted from building muscle (meat), thereby introducing a potential trade-off between desirable production traits and immunocompetence [a functioning immune system].

Germ-free chicks raised in germ-free environments grow faster than chickens in unsanitary environments. Even minute exposures to the normal microbial flora of the gut are enough of an immune stimulus to reduce growth rates significantly. Indeed, even without tissue damage or evidence of disease, the normal, day-to-day functioning of the immune system diverts energy from maximal growth. Germ-free chickens raised in

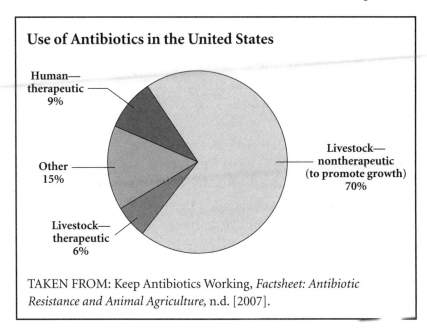

**Use of Antibiotics in the United States**

Human—
therapeutic
9%

Other
15%

Livestock—
therapeutic
6%

Livestock—
nontherapeutic
(to promote growth)
70%

TAKEN FROM: Keep Antibiotics Working, *Factsheet: Antibiotic Resistance and Animal Agriculture*, n.d. [2007].

sanitary laboratory environments and given antibiotics experience no change in growth rates, whereas commercially confined chickens fed antibiotics demonstrate a remarkable spurt in growth.

## Excessive Growth May Hurt Animals

The maintenance of an effective immune system is metabolically very costly. . . . Because antibodies [which fight disease] are made of protein, when the body is producing thousands of antibodies per second, there may be less protein available for growth. Studies show that chickens capable of mounting a decent antibody response have lower weight and lower weight gain than chickens with suboptimal antibody production.

Even relatively insignificant challenges to the immune system can significantly affect growth. Simple vaccinations can result in a greater than 20 percent decline in daily weight gain for farm animals, while increasing protein demands as much as 30 percent, demonstrating the inverse relationship between growth and immunity. In the unhygienic conditions of intensive confinement operations, normal physiological processes like growth may be impaired in light of the infectious load to which animals are exposed. A constant influx of antibiotics may reduce that load.

Unnaturally rapid growth can result in pathological conditions that can further stress the animals. Due to growth-promoting drugs and selective breeding for fast growth, for example, many birds are crippled by painful leg and joint deformities. Animal agriculture industry journal *Feedstuffs* reports that "broilers [chickens raised for meat] now grow so rapidly that the heart and lungs are not developed well enough to support the remainder of the body, resulting in congestive heart failure and tremendous death losses."

"Present production is concentrated in high-volume, crowded, stressful environments, made possible in part by the routine use of antibacterials in feed," the congressional Office of Technology Assessment wrote as far back as 1979. "Thus the current dependency on low-level use of antibacterials to increase or maintain production, while of immediate benefit, also could be the Achilles' heel of present production methods."

## Potential Risks to Human Health

Indiscriminate use of antibiotics may select for drug-resistant pathogens that can affect both human and nonhuman animals. Antibiotics and antibiotic-resistant bacteria can be found in the air, groundwater, and soil around farms and on retail meat, and people can be exposed to these pathogens through infected meat, vegetables fertilized with raw manure, and water supplies contaminated by farm animal waste.

According to the Centers for Disease Control and Prevention (CDC), at least 17 classes of antimicrobials are approved for farm animal growth promotion in the United States, including many families of antibiotics, such as penicillin, tetracycline, and erythromycin, that are critical for treating human disease. As the bacteria become more resistant to the antibiotics fed to chickens and other animals raised for meat, they may become more resistant to the antibiotics needed to treat sick people. Resistance genes that emerge can then be swapped between bacteria. Italian researchers published a DNA fingerprinting study in 2007 showing that these antibiotic-resistance genes could be detected directly in chicken meat and pork.

The world's leading medical, agricultural, and veterinary authorities have reached consensus that antibiotic overuse in animal agriculture is contributing to human public health problems. A joint scientific analysis co-sponsored by the World Health Organization, the Food and Agriculture Organization of the United Nations, and the World Organisation for Animal Health concluded: "There is clear evidence of the human health consequences [from agricultural use of antibiotics, including] infections that would not have otherwise occurred, increased frequency of treatment failures (in some cases death) and increased severity of infections."

This conclusion was derived from multiple lines of evidence including epidemiological studies tracing drug-resistant human infections to specific farm animal production facilities, time lines showing antibiotic-resistant infections in farm animal populations preceding the emergence of the same resistance in humans, and microbial studies showing that antibiotic-resistant bacteria from farm animals not only infect humans, but may transfer that resistance to other bacteria that colonize the human gut. The strongest evidence may be data from Europe's experience, which showed that after antibiotics were banned for growth promotion, there was a subsequent decrease in the levels of antibiotic-resistant bacteria in farm animals, on meat, and within the general human population. According to the head of the CDC's food poisoning surveillance program, "[t]he reason we're seeing an increase in antibiotic resistance in foodborne diseases [in the United States] is because of antibiotic use on the farm."

The Director-General of the World Health Organization fears that this global rise in antibiotic-resistant "superbugs" is threatening to "send the world back to a pre-antibiotic age." As resistant bacteria sweep aside second- and third-line drugs, the CDC's antibiotic-resistance expert says that "we're skating just along the edge." The bacteria seem to be evolving resistance faster than our ability to create new antibiotics. "It takes us 17 years to develop an antibiotic," explains a CDC medical historian. "But a bacterium can develop resistance virtually in minutes. It's as if we're putting our best players on the field, but the bench is getting empty, while their side has an endless supply of new players." Remarked one microbiologist, "Never underestimate an adversary that has a 3.5 billion-year head start."

## Drug-Resistant *Campylobacter* and *Salmonella*

The poultry industry blames the dramatic rise in antibiotic-resistant bacteria on the overprescription of antibiotics by physicians. While doctors undoubtedly play a role, according to the CDC, more and more evidence is accumulating that overuse by animal agriculture industries is particularly worrisome. The September 2005 FDA decision against the Bayer Corporation is illustrative of this point.

Typically, [the bacteria] *Campylobacter* causes only a self-limited diarrheal illness ("stomach flu") that doesn't require antibiotics. If the gastroenteritis is particularly severe, though, or if doctors suspect that the bacteria may be working its way from the gut into the bloodstream, the initial preferred drug is typically a quinolone antibiotic like Cipro [a brand name for ciprofloxacin]. Quinolone antibiotics have been used in human medicine since the 1980s, but widespread antibiotic-resistant *Campylobacter* didn't arise until after quino-lones were licensed for use in chickens in the early 1990s. In countries like Australia, which reserved quinolones exclusively for human use, resistant bacteria are practically unknown.

The FDA concluded that the use of Cipro-like antibiotics in chickens compromised the treatment of nearly 10,000 Americans a year, meaning that thousands infected with *Campylobacter* who sought medical treatment were initially treated with an antibiotic to which the bacteria was resistant, forcing the doctors to switch to more powerful drugs. Studies involving thousands of patients with *Campylobacter* infections showed that this kind of delay in effective treatment led to up to ten times more complications—infections of the brain, the heart, and, the most frequent serious complication they noted, death.

When the FDA announced that it intended to join other countries and ban quinolone antibiotic use on U.S. poultry farms, the drug manufacturer Bayer initiated legal action that succeeded in successfully delaying the process for five years. During that time, Bayer continued to dominate the estimated $15 million a year market and resistance continued to climb.

Antibiotic-resistant *Salmonella* has also led to serious human medical complications. Foodborne *Salmonella* emerged in the U.S. Northeast in the late 1970s and has since spread throughout North America. One theory holds that multidrug-resistant *Salmonella* was disseminated worldwide in the 1980s via contaminated feed made out of farmed fish fed routine antibiotics, a practice condemned by the CDC. The CDC is especially concerned about the recent rapid emergence of a strain resistant to nine separate antibiotics, including the primary treatment used in children. *Salmonella* kills hundreds of Americans every year, hospitalizes thousands, and sickens more than a million.

# Drug Resistant *E. coli* and Influenza

Evidence is mounting that antibiotic-resistant bladder infections may be tied to farm animal drug use as well. Urinary tract infections (UTIs) are the most common bacterial infections in women of all ages, affecting millions every year in the United States. From a physician's perspective, they are getting increasingly difficult to treat, as antibiotic resistance among the chief pathogen, *E[scherichia] coli* [*E. coli*], becomes more common.

Perhaps most familiar is the "Jack-in-the-Box" *E. coli* O157:H7 strain, which starts as hemorrhagic colitis (profuse bloody diarrhea) and can progress to kidney failure, seizures, coma, and death. While *E. coli* O157:H7 remains the leading cause of acute kidney failure in U.S. children, fewer than 100,000 Americans get infected every year and fewer than 100 die. However, millions get "extra-intestinal" *E. coli* infections—urinary tract infections that can invade the bloodstream and are responsible for an estimated 36,000 deaths annually in the United States. While the source of human *E. coli* O157:H7 infection is known to be fecal contamination from the meat, dairy, and egg industries, only recently have scientists traced the path of UTI-type *E. coli*.

Medical researchers at the University of Minnesota took more than 1,000 food samples from multiple retail markets and found evidence of fecal contamination in 69% of the pork and beef tested, and 92% of the poultry samples as evidenced by the presence of *E. coli*. More than 80% of the *E. coli* they recovered from beef, pork, and poultry products were resistant to one or more antibiotics, and greater than half of the samples of poultry bacteria were resistant to more than five drugs. Half of the poultry samples were contaminated with the extra-intestinal pathogenic *E. coli* bacteria, abbreviated ExPEC, further supporting the notion that UTI-type *E. coli* may be foodborne pathogens as well. Scientists suspect that by eating chicken and other animal products, women infect their lower intestinal tract with these antibiotic-resistant bacteria, which can then migrate into their bladder.

Drug resistance is not limited to bacteria. In the 2005 *Washington Post* exposé "Bird Flu Drug Rendered Useless," it was revealed that for years Chinese chicken farmers had been lacing the animals' water supply with the antiviral drug amantadine to prevent economic losses from bird flu. The use of amantadine in the water supply of commercial poultry as prophylaxis against avian influenza was pioneered in the United States after the 1983 outbreak in Pennsylvania. Even then it was shown that drug-resistant mutants arose within nine days of application.

The practice in China has been blamed for the emergence of widespread viral resistance to a life-saving drug that could be used in a human pandemic. "In essence," wrote Frederick Hayden, the Stuart S. Richardson Professor of Clinical Virology in Internal Medicine at the University of Virginia School of Medicine, "this finding means that a whole class of antiviral drugs has been lost as treatment for this virus."

## Calls to Ban the Use of Non-Therapeutic Antibiotics in Animal Agriculture

The European science magazine *New Scientist* editorialized back in 1968 that the use of antibiotics to make animals grow faster "should be abolished altogether." Pleas for caution in the overuse of antibiotics can be traced back farther to the discoverer of penicillin himself, Sir Alexander Fleming, who told the *New York Times* in 1945 that inappropriate use of antibiotics could lead to the selection of "mutant forms" resistant to the drugs. While the European Union banned the use of many medically important antibiotics as farm animal growth promoters years ago, no such comprehensive step has yet taken place in the United States.

The American Medical Association, the American Public Health Association, the Infectious Diseases Society of America, and the American Academy of Pediatrics are among the 350 organizations nationwide that have endorsed efforts to phase out the use of antibiotics important to human medicine as animal feed additives.

In 2001, Donald Kennedy, the editor in chief of *Science*, wrote that the continued feeding of medically important antibiotics to farm animals to promote growth goes against a "strong scientific consensus that it is a bad idea." An editorial the same year in the *New England Journal of Medicine* entitled "Antimicrobial Use in Animal Feed—Time to Stop" came to a similar conclusion.

Despite the consensus among the world's scientific authorities, debate on this issue continues. The editorial board of *Nature Reviews Microbiology* journal offered an explanation: "A major barrier is the fact that many scientists involved in agriculture and food animal producers refuse to accept that the use of antibiotics in livestock has a negative effect on human health. . . . It is understandable that the food-producing industry wishes to protect its interests. However, microbiologists are aware of, and understand, the weight of evidence linking the subtherapeutic use of antibiotics with the emergence of resistant bacteria. Microbiologists also understand the threat that antibiotic resistance poses to public health. As a profession, we must be vocal in supporting any policy that diminishes this threat."

An editorial in the *Western Journal of Medicine* identified erroneous claims made by the pharmaceutical and meat industries and concluded: "The intentional obfuscation of the issue by those with profit in mind is an uncomfortable reminder of the long and ongoing battle to regulate the tobacco industry, with similar dismaying exercises in political and public relations lobbying and even scandal."

This is not the first time the animal agriculture industry has used growth-promoting drugs at the potential expense of human health. Decades ago, the poultry industry pioneered the use of the synthetic growth hormone diethylstilbestrol (DES), despite the fact that it was a known carcinogen. Although some women were prescribed DES during pregnancy—a drug advertised by manufacturers to produce "bigger and stronger babies"—the chief exposure for Americans to DES was through residues in meat. Even after it was proven that women who were exposed to DES gave birth to daughters with high rates of vaginal cancer, the meat industry was able to stonewall a ban on DES in chicken feed for years. According to a Stanford University health policy analyst, only after a study found DES residues in marketed poultry meat at 342,000 times the levels found to be carcinogenic did the FDA finally ban it as a growth promoter in poultry in 1979.

Dr. Kennedy, who served as commissioner of the U.S. Food and Drug Administration from 1977 to 1979, describes the antibiotic debate as a "struggle between good science and strong politics." When meat production interests pressured Congress to shelve an FDA proposal to limit the practice, Kennedy concluded: "Science lost."

## Financial Ramifications

The U.S. Government Accountability Office [GAO] released a 2004 report on the use of antibiotics as growth promoters in farm animals. Though the GAO acknowledged that "[m]any studies have found that the use of antibiotics in animals poses significant risks for human health," a ban could, in part, result in a "reduction of profits" for the industry. The report published rears that even a partial ban might "increase costs to producers, decrease production, and increase retail prices to consumers."

An unsubstantiated industry estimate of the costs associated with a total ban on the widespread feeding of antibiotics to farm animals in the United States would be an increase in the price of poultry from 1 to 2 cents per pound and the price of pork or beef between 3 to 6 cents a pound. This could cost the average U.S. meat-eating consumer as much as $9.72 a year.

Antibiotic-resistant infections in the United States from all sources cost an estimated $30 billion every year and kill 90,000 people.

A major analysis of the elimination of growth-promoting antibiotics in Denmark, one of the world's largest pork producers, showed that the move led to a marked reduction in bacterial antibiotic resistance without significant adverse effects on productivity. U.S. industry, however, has argued that the Danish experience cannot be extrapolated to the United States. This led Johns Hopkins University researchers to carry out an economic analysis based on data from Perdue, one of the largest poultry producers in the United States.

The Johns Hopkins University Bloomberg School of Public Health study, published in 2007, examined data from seven million chickens and concluded that the use of antibiotics in chicken feed *increases* costs of poultry production. "Contrary to the long-held belief that a ban against GPAs [growth-promoting antibiotics] would raise costs to producers and consumers," the researchers concluded, "these results using a large-scale industry study demonstrate the opposite." They found that the conditions in Perdue's facilities were such that antibiotics did accelerate the birds' growth rates, but the money saved was insufficient to offset the cost of the antibiotics themselves. Growth-promoting antibiotics may end up costing producers more in the end than if they hadn't used antibiotics at all. A similar study at Kansas State University also showed no economic benefits from feeding antibiotics to "finishing" pigs [adult pigs].

The practice of feeding antibiotics to farm animals to promote faster growth is being phased out in countries around the world to protect the public's health. Given the lack of demonstrable benefits, the U.S. meat industry should heed the call of the U.S. public health community and global authorities to follow this lead. With few, if any, new classes of antibiotics in clinical development, an expert on antibiotic resistance at the Institute for Agriculture and Trade Policy warned that "we're sacrificing a future where antibiotics will work for treating sick people by squandering them today for animals that are not sick at all."

*"From 1992 . . . to 2008, overall antibiotic use in swine production declined substantially—by over 50 percent—as a result of the ban on growth promoters in Denmark. In addition, there were no serious long-term effects on swine health."*

# Reducing Antibiotics on Farms Has Proved Successful

## Pew Charitable Trusts

*The Pew Charitable Trusts is an independent, nonprofit organization that works to improve public policy, inform the public, and stimulate civic life. In the following viewpoint, the organization argues that the elimination of antibiotics to promote growth in livestock did not have any negative health or economic consequences in Denmark. In addition, the ban reduced antibiotic resistance in animals and appears to also have reduced antibiotic resistance in humans. The viewpoint concludes that a ban on antibiotics for growth in livestock should be adopted in the United States as well.*

As you read, consider the following questions:

1. How does Denmark regulate all uses of antibiotics in food animals, according to the viewpoint?
2. According to the viewpoint, what changes in animal husbandry did the Danish industry have to institute following the ban on AGPs?
3. The viewpoint says that banning AGPs cost pig and chicken producers how much?

In human medicine, antibiotic use is generally confined to treatment of illness. In contrast, antibiotics and other antimicrobials (drugs that kill microorganisms like bacteria) often are routinely given to food animals in the U.S. in order to grow animals faster and to compensate for unsanitary conditions on many industrial farms. Bacteria exposed to antibiotics at low doses for prolonged periods can develop antibiotic resistance—a dangerous trait enabling bacteria to survive and grow instead of being inhibited or destroyed by therapeutic doses of a drug. Since many of the classes of antibiotics used in food animal production also are important in human medicine, resistance that begins on the farm can lead to a serious public health problem.

## Denmark and Farm Antibiotics

Recognizing the potential for a health crisis, Denmark stopped the administration of antibiotics used for growth promotion (i.e., non-medical uses) in broiler chickens [chickens raised for meat] and adult swine (finishers) in 1998, and in young swine (weaners) in 1999. Today [2008] in Denmark, all uses of antibiotics in food animals must be accompanied by a prescription in a valid veterinarian-client-patient relationship, and veterinarians cannot profit from the sale of antibiotics. In addition, farmers, veterinarians and pharmacies must report the use and sale of antibiotics, and farm inspections are conducted regularly. Although the U.S. food animal production and animal drug industries often claim that the ban was costly and ineffective, the World Health Organization (WHO) found that the Danish ban reduced human health risk without significantly harming animal health or farmers' incomes. In fact, Danish government and industry data show that livestock and poultry production has increased since the ban, while antibiotic resistance has declined on farms and in meat.

In 2003, the WHO published a study entitled "Impacts of Antimicrobial Growth Promoter Termination in Denmark," which culminated their review of Denmark's elimination of antimicrobial growth promoters (AGPs) in food animal production—a ban that was five years old at the time. The goals set forth by WHO included assessing the impact of the ban on: antibiotic resistance in humans; human health; animal health and welfare; the environment and animal production. The report focused particularly on swine and broiler chickens, and based its study on data from the Danish [Integrated] Antimicrobial Resistance Monitoring and Research Program (DANMAP) and VETSTAT, as well as national experts' working papers. VETSTAT, a special antimicrobial use monitoring program originating in 2000, is a prescription-based initiative that collects information on veterinary prescriptions from pharmacies, vet practices and feed mills.

Researchers with the Danish Veterinary and Food Administration, the Danish Medicines Agency, the Technical University of Denmark and the State Serum Institute have been compiling, analyzing and publishing data on antibiotic use in food animals since the early 1990s. In addition, they have studied antibiotic resistance in animals and food since the mid-1990s and in humans since the early 2000s. DANMAP publishes this data in an annual report available online. Many of the report writers and their colleagues also have published findings of the Denmark ban in independent scientific literature. Additional journal articles have been published comparing the impacts of the AGP ban in Denmark to similar bans in Sweden and Norway, which also were successful in reducing antibiotic use and antibiotic resistance.

## Human Health, Animal Welfare, and the Environment

From 1992, the peak of AGP usage in pigs, to 2008, overall antibiotic use in swine production declined substantially—by over 50 percent—as a result of the ban on growth promoters in Denmark. In addition, there were no serious long-term effects on swine health.

U.S. industry has expressed alarm over increased treatment of diarrhea and a rise in mortality in weaner pigs in the few years immediately after the ban. The WHO found that diarrhea in young pigs did increase following the ban, creating a short-term need to increase therapeutic antibiotic use. However, levels of diarrhea treatment began to decline after seven months and were back to the pre-ban levels after one year, and weaner mortality has improved considerably in recent years.

According to Danish industry representatives, minor changes in animal husbandry, such as more frequent cleaning of housing, improved ventilation, later weaning, additional space for animal movement, as well as experimenting with feed quality and additives made up for the lack of routine antibiotics on most farms. Today, Danish industry considers farmers to be "adapted" to the ban.

The WHO determined that Denmark's AGP ban achieved its public health goal of reducing resistance in food animals in order to prevent related human resistance from emerging. Extensive data showed that the ban drastically reduced the antibiotic-resistant *Enterococci* in animals, a bacterium that can lead to human illnesses such as urinary tract infections, intra-abdominal infections and surgical wound infections.

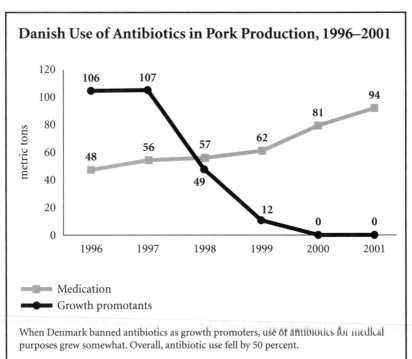

## Danish Use of Antibiotics in Pork Production, 1996–2001

When Denmark banned antibiotics as growth promoters, use of antibiotics for medical purposes grew somewhat. Overall, antibiotic use fell by 50 percent.

TAKEN FROM: Helen H. Jensen and Dermot J. Hayes, "Antibiotics Restrictions: Taking Stock of Denmark's Experience," *Iowa Ag Review Online*, Summer 2003, 9:3.

However, in 2003 the WHO could not determine the ban's direct and total effect on antimicrobial resistance in humans because of limited data. Newer monitoring data, however, show that human resistance trends appear to be mirroring the decline in on-farm use of antibiotics—a positive indicator for public health. Today, the Danish Ministry of Food, Agriculture and Fisheries reports, "The stop for use of different nontherapeutic antibiotic growth promoters . . . has resulted in a major reduction in antimicrobial resistance as measured among several different bacterial species in food animals and food."

# Economic Impacts and Production Trends

According to the Danish Ministry of Food, Agriculture and Fisheries:

> In Denmark the termination of nontherapeutic use of antibiotics for growth promotion has not caused any negative impact on the animal production. The Danish animal food industry has continued to improve its productivity and to increase its output.

Following the ban in Denmark, swine production has increased by nearly 50 percent since 1992. In addition, the average number of pigs born per sow has increased (a key indicator of swine health), and the average daily gain of weaners and finishers has increased since the ban. While weaner mortality increased for a few years after the ban (by less than one percent, according to the WHO), it was already increasing for several years before the ban, and has been dramatically decreasing in recent years, indicating "no effect of the termination." Broiler production rates and mortality were not affected by the ban.

The WHO found that the AGP ban had several minor impacts on the hog life cycle that in turn affected production. It took close to an extra day and a half to reach slaughter weight, while it took almost three days for weaners to reach their goal weight. However, Danish Pig Production (an industry group) suspects that the total effect of the ban may have been more like 1.6 days of added growth time over a pig's lifetime, with most impact felt during the weaner period. Overall, the WHO agreed with Danish government and industry findings that the ban did not have a direct impact on the growth rate and increased mortality of finishers. The study likewise found no impacts on broiler chicken mortality or weight gain changes in broilers attributable to the ban.

Tied closely to the reduced growth rate in hogs are the economic costs associated with the ban. In general, the WHO report found that overall economic impacts were minimal. Costs varied among farmers, but may have included the costs associated with modifying the production system; decreased feed efficiency; reduced growth/increased mortality in weaners and increased use of therapeutic antimicrobials or the purchase of alternatives to AGPs. The WHO panel found that each pig produced cost the producer 7.75 DKK [Danish krone] ($1.09 in 2003) more than before the ban, translating to a comprehensive production cost increase of just over one percent. The WHO found no net increase in costs to poultry production.

Overall, the combination of production impacts on hogs and poultry farmers caused very minimal loss (0.03 percent) to Denmark's economy.

## Ending AGP Use in the U.S.

In Denmark, like in the U.S., the trend in food animal production favors an industrial model with fewer farms producing more food animals per farm. The WHO report has clearly concluded that eliminating AGPs in such a system does not have significantly adverse economic consequences.

Other recent studies agree with such findings. A peer-reviewed economic report produced for the Pew Commission on Industrial Farm [Animal] Production by the University of Tennessee's Agricultural Policy Analysis Center found that when accounting for societal and environmental costs, industrial swine farming methods are usually more expensive than alternative methods such as hoop barns [tubular tent-like barns], which typically do not involve the use of antibiotics for growth promotion. An economic analysis conducted on the U.S. poultry industry by researchers from Johns Hopkins University also was consistent with the WHO's findings. The researchers concluded that the costs of production are reduced when AGPs are not used. In their research, the increased cost of feed containing antibiotics outweighed the costs associated with the alternative, i.e., the increased amount of feed needed combined with the slightly increased mortality, variability in weight gain and increased condemnation rates (chickens rejected at slaughter due to illness or disease).

There is current [2008] legislation that would address the routine use of antibiotics on industrial farms. The Preservation of Antibiotics for Medical Treatment Act would withdraw the use of seven classes of antibiotics vitally important to human health from food animal production unless animals or herds are sick or unless drug companies can prove that their nontherapeutic use does not harm human health by contributing to antibiotic resistance.

The WHO's report on the termination of AGPs in food animals in Denmark concludes with final remarks summarizing their findings: the use of antimicrobials for the sole purpose of growth promotion can be discontinued in countries with "similar animal production conditions," and the routine nontherapeutic use of antimicrobials should never be a substitute for good animal health management. The ban in Denmark led to fewer animals being given antimicrobials and those who are given them for disease treatment have a shortened exposure time. The termination of AGPs affected weaner pigs more than finishers but had small overall negative economic impact in the swine industry, while there was no negative impact on broilers. Overall, the ban phasing out the nontherapeutic use of antibiotics for growth promotion has not caused any negative impact on food animal production in Denmark. In fact, the industry's productivity has increased as well as its output.

*"According to published news reports, the number of pigs that died from illnesses increased by 25 percent from 1995 to 2005."*

# Reducing Antibiotics on Farms Has Proved Detrimental

## Ohio Pork Producers Council

*The Ohio Pork Producers Council is an industry organization that promotes the safe consumption of pork. In the following viewpoint, the organization argues that the Danish experience with banning antibiotics for growth promotion on farms was not safe or effective. The viewpoint says that the ban did not significantly reduce the use of antibiotics, since more medical antibiotics had to be prescribed. In addition, the viewpoint claims, no health benefits to humans were proven. The viewpoint also says that a similar ban would cause serious economic damage in the United States.*

As you read, consider the following questions:

1. What is the precautionary principle of risk management, according to this viewpoint?

2. What method does this viewpoint say the FDA uses in the United States to determine whether antibiotic use is safe?

3. Why does the viewpoint say that a ban in the United States would create problems that were not observed in Denmark?

Lessons learned when Denmark removed antibiotics as growth promoters (AGPs) provide a good example of consequences from restrictions on antibiotic usage in the livestock industry;;;.

*Q: What is the "Danish Experience"?*

A: In 1998, the Danish government instituted a voluntary ban on the use of antibiotic growth promotants (AGPs) during the finishing stage of pork production. The Danish pork industry agreed to the ban. The use of AGPs was withdrawn for all swine in 2000.

*Q: Why was the ban imposed?*

A: Key drivers of the ban were an increase in antibiotic imports into Denmark, the resulting political opinions and a concern from the scientific community that human health could be adversely affected by the use of antibiotics, including AGPs.[1] The ban invoked the precautionary principle for risk management that says that if any possibility exists that human health can be negatively impacted, no matter how remote, regulators should remove it by restricting food industry practices.[2] There was an assumption that banning AGP use would lead to a decreased amount of antibiotic use in agriculture and a decreased risk to human health from bacteria resistant to antibiotics.

*Q: Did Denmark ban the use of all antibiotics in pork production?*

A: No. A ban was enacted for the use of antibiotics as growth promotants for finisher [adult] pigs in 1998 and for nursery pigs in 1999. Antibiotics, including those used in feed and water for controlling and treating disease were not banned, and indeed are now being used more frequently than before the ban.

*Q: What was the result of the ban at the finishing stage?*

A: Initially, farmers generally reported few health problems. Some farms noticed negative impacts in average daily gain and mortality. Many farms have adjusted production practices to address these negative impacts and some farms have not been able to.

*Q: Was the result of the ban at the weaning stage similar to the finishing stage?*

A: No. Farmers noted an increase in piglet diarrhea, higher mortality rates, decreased weight gains, and greater weight variations.[3] According to published news reports[4], the number of pigs that died from illnesses increased by 25 percent from 1995 to 2005. These effects have still not been totally resolved.

*Q: Was there a decrease in antibiotic usage?*

A: Yes and no. Veterinarians resorted to significant increases in the usage of therapeutic antibiotics to combat rising health issues and declining production levels. While total antibiotic use has decreased somewhat, therapeutic usage of antibiotics has surpassed the level of AGP usage prior to the ban.[5]

*Q: How was human health affected by the ban?*

A: There have been no proven human health benefits from the ban on AGPs in pork production. One potential negative consequence is that resistance to tetracyclines [a group of antibiotics] in *Salmonella* [a dangerous bacteria] causing human infection has actually increased since the ban.[6]

*Q: Have more restrictions on AGP usage been imposed in Denmark and elsewhere in Europe since the late 1990s?*

A: In January 2006, the European Union banned all remaining antimicrobial growth promoters on a precautionary basis. While there is no direct evidence of antibiotic resistance problems in humans resulting from AGP usage in pork production, the European Union favors the Precautionary Principle and removing any theoretical risk of that occurring.[7]

*Q: What is the U.S. approach to addressing risk to human health from antibiotic use in agriculture?*

A: The Food and Drug Administration's [FDA's] Center for Veterinary Medicine . . . uses a risk assessment approach to determine human health risks of antibiotic use in food animals on a case-by-case basis. FDA's Guidance #152 uses a scientific framework to assess the human health effects of veterinary use of antibiotics. The Guidance requires antibiotic manufacturers to provide information to the FDA showing that a proposed animal drug will not harm public health.

*Q: What would the financial impact of such a ban be on U.S. pork producers?*

A: An Iowa State University economist estimates production costs could increase up to $6.00 per animal in the first year following a ban. . . .

Over 10 years, the total projected cost of such a ban would exceed $1.1 billion. Consumers could expect to pay about 2 percent more for pork products.[8]

*Q: What should we learn from the Danish experience?*

A: Evidence shows such a ban will cause animal health and well-being problems. There is no evidence that such a ban would protect public health. The current FDA risk assessment on a drug-by-drug basis provides a scientifically sound process to protect human health and animal well-being. Other differences between the United States and Denmark could create additional problems in the United States that were not observed in Denmark. For example:

- U.S. veterinarians, by law, don't have the prescription ability to change medication dosages in feed like the Danish veterinarians do. We would have to use more antibiotics in the feed to accomplish the same disease prevention during stress or disease outbreaks that we now can accomplish using smaller amounts.

- Unlike the cooperative system used in Denmark, the U.S. marketing system is competitive. Danish producers have the ability to negotiate price and make up for the increased production costs due to the decision to ban these uses. U.S. producers will not have this ability to recoup the predicted higher production costs.

*Q: What is the U.S. pork industry doing to ensure appropriate uses of antibiotics and to safeguard public health?*

A: The National Pork Board has launched a program called Take Care—Use Antibiotics Responsibly. It has three main goals for pork producers:

1. To educate producers about the responsible use of antibiotics.
2. To raise producers' awareness of the importance of using antibiotics responsibly and the impact of this on animal and public health.
3. To demonstrate to customers and consumers, pork producers' commitment to preserving public health, animal health, and animal well-being through the responsible use of antibiotics.

This program includes principles and guidelines that producers and their veterinarians can use together to better manage the use of antibiotics and will become part of the Pork Quality Assurance Plus program in 2008. It is a proactive approach to the responsible use of antibiotics within the pork industry.

## Notes

1. Casewell, Friis, Marco, McMullin, Phillips. The European Ban on Growth-Promoting Antibiotics and Emerging Consequences for Human and Animal Health. *Journal of Antimicrobial Chemotherapy.* 2003.
2. Hayes, Jensen, Fabios. Technology Choice and the Economic Effects of a Ban on the Use of Antimicrobial Feed Additives in Swine Rations. *Food Control.* 2002.
3. Steinhart, McMullen. Iowa State University Extension. 2005.
4. Agence France-Presse. World-Leading Pork Exporter Denmark Sees Sharp Increase in Pig Mortality. Copenhagen Business Online. 2005. http://archive.wn.com/2005/09/06/1400/copenhagenbusiness/.
5. DANMAP 2005. www.danmap.org.
6. World Health Organization. Impacts of Antimicrobial Growth Promoter Termination in Denmark. Online. 2002. http://whqlibdoc.who.int/hq/2003/WHO_CDS_CPE_ZFK_2003.1.pdf.
7. Hayes, Jensen, Fabios. Technology Choice and the Economic Effects of a Ban on the Use of Antimicrobial Feed Additives in Swine Rations. *Food Control.* 2002.
8. Hayes, Jensen, Backstrom. National Pork Board Final Research Grant Report—Analysis of a More Restricted Antimicrobial Access Policy in Pork Production, Funded Research Project #02-104.

"Scientists believe antibiotics also may have contributed to the explosive rise in asthma and allergies in children over the last 20 years."

# Antibiotic Use on Farms May Affect Crops

*Matthew Cimitile*

*Matthew Cimitile is an intern at* Environmental Health News. *In the following viewpoint, he reports that some vegetables absorb antibiotics when grown in soil fertilized with animal manure. Though the amount of antibiotics absorbed in this way is small, there may be health implications. For example, Cimitile notes, antibiotics in vegetables may contribute to the development of disease-resistant bacteria and possibly to the increase in children's asthma and allergies. Cimitile also points out that organic farming uses manure and that organic vegetables may therefore also be laced with antibiotics.*

As you read, consider the following questions:

1. Which vegetables are not processed, only washed, and would therefore probably retain antibiotics, according to Cimitile's reporting?

2. According to Cimitile, what volume of antibiotics is given to animals for agricultural purposes in the United States, and how much has this increased since the 1980s?

3. What does the viewpoint say can be done to manure to help reduce antibiotics?

For half a century, meat producers have fed antibiotics to farm animals to increase their growth and stave off infections. Now scientists have discovered that those drugs are sprouting up in unexpected places.

## From Livestock Manure to Vegetables

Vegetables such as corn, potatoes and lettuce absorb antibiotics when grown in soil fertilized with livestock manure, according to tests conducted at the University of Minnesota.

Today, close to 70 percent of the total antibiotics and related drugs produced in the United States are fed to cattle, pigs and poultry, according to the Union of Concerned Scientists. Although this practice sustains a growing demand for meat, it also generates public health fears associated with the expanding presence of antibiotics in the food chain.

People have long been exposed to antibiotics in meat and milk. Now, the new research shows that they also may be ingesting them from vegetables, perhaps even ones grown on organic farms.

The Minnesota researchers planted corn, green onion and cabbage in manure-treated soil in 2005 to evaluate the environmental impacts of feeding antibiotics to livestock. Six weeks later, the crops were analyzed and found to absorb chlortetracycline, a drug widely used to treat diseases in livestock. In another study in 2007, corn, lettuce and potato were planted in soil treated with liquid hog manure. They, too, accumulated concentrations of an antibiotic, named sulfamethazine, also commonly used in livestock.

As the amount of antibiotics in the soil increased, so too did the levels taken up by the corn, potatoes and other plants.

## Health Effects Are Unknown

"Around 90 percent of these drugs that are administered to animals end up being excreted either as urine or manure," said Holly Dolliver, a member of the Minnesota research team and now a professor of crop and soil sciences at the University of Wisconsin–River Falls. "A vast majority of that manure is then used as an important input for 9.2 million hectares of (U.S.) agricultural land."

Manure, widely used as a substitute for chemical fertilizer, adds nutrients that help plants grow. It is often used in organic farming.

The scientists found that although their crops were only propagated in greenhouses for six weeks—far less than a normal growing season—antibiotics were absorbed readily into their leaves. If grown for a full season, drugs most likely would find their way into parts of plants that humans eat, said Dolliver.

Less than 0.1 percent of antibiotics applied to soil were absorbed into the corn, lettuce and other plants. Though a tiny amount, health implications for people consuming such small, cumulative doses are largely unknown.

"The antibiotic accumulation in plants is just another negative consequence of our animal agriculture industry and not surprising given the quantity fed to livestock," said Steve Roach, public health program director for the nonprofit Food Animal Concerns Trust.

For highly processed plants such as corn, the drugs would most likely be removed, added Dolliver. But many food crops such as spinach and lettuce are not processed, only washed, allowing antibiotics to remain.

"Nobody particularly eats corn or soybean directly," said Satish Gupta, a University of Minnesota professor of soil science and study leader. "But there are crops I am much more worried about, like cabbage and lettuce, because these are leaves we eat directly and consume raw."

One finding that particularly worries food scientists is the accumulation of antibiotics within potato tubers. Tubers are an enlarged, underground stem that uptake and store nutrients from the soil. In crops like potatoes, carrots and radishes, it is the part humans eat.

"Since these tubers and root crops are in direct contact with the soil they may show a greater propensity for (antibiotic) uptake," said Gupta.

## Resistant Bacteria and an Increase in Allergies

Health officials fear that eating vegetables and meat laced with drugs meant to treat infections can promote resistant strains of bacteria in food and the environment.

Roach said "the clearest public health implication" from treating livestock with antibiotics is the development of resistant bacteria that reduces the effectiveness of human medicine. Past studies have shown overuse of antibiotics reduces their ability to cure infections. Over time, certain antibiotics are rendered ineffective.

Scientists believe antibiotics also may have contributed to the explosive rise in asthma and allergies in children over the last 20 years. Researchers at Henry Ford Hospital in Detroit, following 448 children from birth for seven years, reported that children who received antibiotics within their first six months had a higher risk of developing allergies and asthma.

Such health concerns led the European Union in 2006 to ban antibiotic use as feed additives for promoting livestock growth. But in the United States, nearly 25 million pounds of antibiotics per year, up from 16 million in the mid 1980s, are given to healthy animals for agriculture purposes, according to a 2000 report by the Union of Concerned Scientists.

Livestock producers contend that the spread of resistant strains of bacteria stems from the overuse of all medicines to treat infectious diseases in both humans and animals. Removal of antibiotics, they say, would only lead to increased disease in animals and reduction in food safety.

Tainted manure can impact more than just the soil. Once applied to the land, antibiotics can infiltrate water supplies as [the water] seeps through the soil into aquifers or spills into surface water due to runoff, explained Dolliver.

"The other thing to remember is that the field is not a sterile environment. Mice, rabbits and foxes traverse farmland while other animals graze, all with the potential to become vectors for the resistant bacteria organisms and spread it throughout different animal populations," said Pat Millner, a U.S. Department of Agriculture [USDA] microbiologist based in Maryland.

The presence of antibiotics within the food chain is likely to increase as the U.S. Food and Drug Administration [FDA] has permitted greater use of controversial drugs on farm animals. For example, this past October [2008], the FDA dropped plans to halt use of cefquinome, a potent antibiotic, after it said in July it would push against its use in animals.

## Antibiotics in Organic Farming

While there are restrictions on use of raw manure in U.S. organic farming because of concern over bacteria, no such rules are in place regarding antibiotics or hormones. Not all organic growers use manure with antibiotics, but many do, said Gupta. Even if a product has the USDA organic label, it still might harbor traces of antibiotics.

High-temperature composting of manure, designed to kill pathogens, is required for crops certified under the USDA organic label. That could eliminate some antibiotics. But others

## Antibiotics May Contribute to Asthma

In a cohort of 13,116 children born in Manitoba [Canada] in 1995, we found an association between antibiotic use in the first year of life and asthma at age 7 years. Children receiving more than four courses of antibiotics were at 1.5 times the risk of having asthma develop than were children not receiving antibiotics. . . . Moreover, the association was observed for antibiotic use in the treatment of children for non-respiratory tract infections, for which the risk of asthma was doubled.

*Anita L. Kozyrskyj, Pierre Ernst, and Allan B. Becker, "Increased Risk of Childhood Asthma from Antibiotic Use in Early Life," CHEST, vol. 131, no. 6, June 2007, pp. 1753-1759. http://chestjournal.chestpubs.org.*

are resistant, according to a study by Dolliver and Gupta published last year. Growers are not required to monitor crops for the drugs.

"Antibiotic uptake by plants may be of particular concern to organic crop producers. . . . To our knowledge, there is no current plan or standardized methodology for monitoring antibiotics in animal manure, which is often obtained from non-organic farms where antibiotics are commonly used," Dolliver said in the 2007 study.

Added Gupta, "We urgently need to find some way to put guidelines in place on organic food regarding these chemicals."

Gupta said all growers should be told that composting manure can help reduce antibiotics. Composting decays piles of food or manure as microbes decompose organic matter using oxygen to survive, grow and reproduce. Heating up the material creates conditions conducive for bacteria to break down antibiotics and pathogens.

A pilot study by USDA scientists in Maryland added straw to a beef cattle manure pile, heating up the dense material while allowing spaces for air to penetrate. The higher temperatures sped up the decaying process of harmful substances.

"The process happens very rapidly, in this study it took about 10 days," said Millner. "This is not too surprising since antibiotics are not a thermally stable chemical compound."

In another study, the same researchers who discovered the uptake of antibiotics by plants tested four of these drugs to determine how effective composting would be in reducing harmful chemicals in turkey manure. After 25 days using a combination of natural heat generated by microbial activity, three of the four antibiotics broke down under the high energy conditions created, said Dolliver.

Composting reduced concentrations of three antibiotics by 54 percent to 99 percent, although one drug, sulfamethazine, did not degrade at all, according to their study, published in May in the *Journal of Environmental Quality*.

"These findings suggest manure management can be an important strategy for reducing the overall impact for these compounds making their way into the environment," said Dolliver.

Many questions still remain. Currently, projects are under way to grow crops for a full season in antibiotic-laced manure, to grow them in fields rather than greenhouses and to analyze the concentrations and locations of the antibiotics within the plants. Researchers also want to determine which antibiotics are more likely to be picked up, which plants are more prone to uptake, what composting methods are most effective in reducing harmful material in manure and what antibiotics may be resistant to composting.

There are serious societal implications regarding the discoveries already made and the questions yet to be answered, Gupta concluded.

"We are a chemical society and humans are the main user of pharmaceutical products," said Gupta. "We need a better understanding of what takes place when chemicals are applied to sources of food and must be more vigilant about regulating what we use to grow food and what we put in our bodies."

> *"Opponents fear bacteria inside the guts of animals fed the GM potato—which can cause human diseases—may develop resistance to antibiotics."*

# Antibiotic Resistance Genes in GM Crops May Be Dangerous

## Martin Hickman and Genevieve Roberts

*Martin Hickman is the consumer affairs correspondent for the* Independent; *Genevieve Roberts has written for the* Independent. *In the following viewpoint, they report on tension over the introduction of a genetically modified potato in Europe. The potato includes a gene that can resist antibiotics. Opponents of the potato worry that the gene may get into the gut bacteria of animals that eat the potato. The concern is that this bacteria, which can cause diseases in humans, may become resistant to antibiotics.*

As you read, consider the following questions:

1. Which countries plan to use the GM potato and which attacked the adoption of the potato, according to this viewpoint?

2. How many people does this viewpoint say are infected by tuberculosis every year?

3. What would stringent controls on the potatoes ensure, according to the EU?

The introduction of a genetically modified [GM] potato in Europe risks the development of human diseases that fail to respond to antibiotics, it was claimed last night [March 3, 2010].

German chemical giant BASF this week won approval from the European Commission [EC] for commercial growing of a starchy potato with a gene that could resist antibiotics—useful in the fight against illnesses such as tuberculosis.

Farms in Germany, Sweden, the Netherlands and the Czech Republic may plant the potato for industrial use, with part of the tuber fed to cattle, according to BASF, which fought a 13-year battle to win approval for Amflora [the GM potato]. But other EU member states, including Italy and Austria and anti-GM campaigners angrily attacked the move, claiming it could result in a health disaster.

During the regulatory tussle over the potato, the EU's [European Union's] pharmaceutical regulator had expressed concern about its potential to interfere with the efficacy of antibiotics on infections that develop multiple resistance to other antibiotics, a growing problem in human and veterinary medicine. Amflora contains a gene that produces an enzyme which generally confers resistance to several antibiotics, including kanamycin, neomycin, butirosin, and gentamicin.

The antibiotics could become "extremely important" to treat otherwise multi-resistant infections and tuberculosis [TB], the European Medicines [Agency] (EMA) warned. Drug resistance is part of the explanation for the resurgence of TB, which infects eight million people worldwide every year.

"In the absence of an effective therapy, infectious Multiple Drug Resistant TB [MDR-TB] patients will continue to spread the disease, producing new infections with MDR-TB strains," an EMA spokesman said. "Until we introduce a new drug with demonstrated activity against MDR strains, this aspect of the TB epidemic could explode at an exponential level."

After member states became deadlocked on the potato's approval, the European Commission approved it for use in industries such as paper production, saying it would save energy, water and chemicals. Once the starch has been removed, the skins can be fed to animals, whose meat would not have to be labelled as GM.

The EC, whose decision was backed by the European Food Safety Authority (EFSA), said there was no good reason for withholding approval. Health and consumer policy commissioner John Dalli said: "Responsible innovation will be my guiding principle when dealing with innovative technologies."

"Stringent" controls would ensure none of the tubers were left in the ground, ensuring altered genes did not escape into the environment. Opponents fear bacteria inside the guts of animals fed the GM potato—which can cause human diseases—may develop resistance to antibiotics.

Some member states were furious. "Not only are we against this decision, but we want to underscore that we will not allow the questioning of member states' sovereignty on this matter," said Italy's Agriculture Minister, Luca Zaia. Austria said it would ban cultivation of the potato within its borders, while France said it would ask an expert panel for further research.

Campaigners accused Brussels of failing to follow the precautionary principle [the principle that the burden of proof is on those who are trying to show that an action will *not* harm the public]. Friends of the Earth's Heike Moldenhauer said: "The commissioner, whose job is to protect consumers, has, in one of his first decisions, ignored public opinion and safety concerns to please the world's biggest chemical company."

Campaigners suspect Brussels [the seat of the European Union] is in favour of the widespread planting of GM crops despite opposition by some member states. Yesterday it also announced its intention to allow states more leeway in backing GM organisms.

| "Scientists have been unable to demonstrate the transfer of antibiotic resistance genes from biotech crops to bacteria even under the most favorable conditions."

# Antibiotic Resistance Genes in GM Crops Are Not Dangerous

*Bruce M. Chassy*

*Bruce M. Chassy is professor of food microbiology and nutrition at the University of Illinois at Urbana-Champaign. In the following viewpoint, he explains that antibiotic resistance genes are used in genetically modified plants to help researchers identify, or mark, when a modification has been successful. Chassy says that, despite many tests, antibiotic resistance genes have never been found to transfer from crops to bacteria. He concludes that antibiotic resistance genes in crops will not create antibiotic-resistant bacteria and therefore pose no danger to humans.*

As you read, consider the following questions:

1. What is a callus, according to Chassy?

Bruce M. Chassy, "Will Agricultural Biotechnology Lead to the Spread of Antibiotic Resistance?" *Agricultural Biotechnology*, March 8, 2008. Copyright © 2008 Agricultural Biotechnology Communicators. Reproduced by permission of the author.

2. What two simple guidelines does Chassy say the developers of biotech crops must follow with regard to marker genes?

3. What does Chassy suggest people should worry about instead of antibiotic resistance genes in biotech crops?

Introducing a new trait to plants, by inserting DNA into target plant cells, can be a "long shot." Sometimes only one in a thousand—or even one in a million—plant cells will take up the inserted DNA and incorporate the new gene. So biotechnologists need a "marker" to show up when they have hit the target.

## Antibiotic Resistance Is a Useful Marker

One such marker is antibiotic resistance. If genes for antibiotic resistance are linked to genes for the desirable trait, researchers can single out plant cells that have been transformed successfully by exposing all cells to an antibiotic. Plants cells that successfully incorporated the combined genes (for the desirable plant trait and for antibiotic resistance) will survive the antibiotic test and will grow into little mounds of transformed plant cells called a *callus*. Then the researchers can isolate cells from the callus and regenerate whole plants with the newly introduced, desired trait. This means, however, that some new varieties of plants with desirable traits, such as insect resistance or herbicide tolerance, may also carry a new gene for antibiotic resistance.

*Question: Will biotechnology promote the spread of antibiotic resistance?*

Answer: It is natural to wonder if growing millions of acres of biotech crops containing antibiotic resistance marker genes will add to the already growing problem of antibiotic resistance. Scientists and regulatory agencies around the world look very thoroughly at this question before such crops are approved. In order to avoid this possibility, the developers of biotech crops have been asked to follow some simple guidelines with respect to marker genes. The first is that they should not use an antibiotic resistance marker gene that is not already widespread in nature. Secondly, markers that encode resistance to very important and powerful antibiotics, for which there are no good alternatives in medicine or veterinary practice, should not be used at all.

*Aren't there alternatives to using antibiotic resistance as a transformation marker?*

Sometimes other marker systems can be used to detect the desired new varieties, for example, herbicide tolerance genes can be used to make transformed plants resistant to herbicide. Successful transformants can be detected by their ability to grow on media containing herbicides. Scientists are developing other marker systems that do not use antibiotic resistance genes. The trend today is for newly introduced varieties to not contain antibiotic resistance marker genes.

## No Real Threat

*But you're talking about plant systems. What does antibiotic resistance in plants have to do with human health and the bacteria that "bug" us?*

While it is plausible that the DNA from antibiotic marker genes could be taken up by bacteria in the soil and passed onto other bacteria that then become antibiotic-resistant pathogens that cause infection in humans, research has demonstrated that it is highly unlikely. In fact, despite repeated attempts over the last decade, scientists have been unable to demonstrate the transfer of antibiotic resistance genes from biotech crops to bacteria even under the most favorable conditions.

## Use of Antibiotic Resistance Genes in GM Plants Has Shown No Risk

- The probability of a successful transfer of an antibiotic resistance gene to a bacterium is very low. Estimates from laboratory experiments place the probability at anywhere from 1:10,000,000,000,000 to 1:1,000,000,000,000,000,000,000,000,000.

- Whenever we eat fruits and vegetables we are eating antibiotic-resistant microorganisms from the soil. This has no known negative effects.

*GMO Compass, "Antibiotic Resistance Genes: A Threat?" December 12, 2006. www.gmo-compass.org.*

However, there is a second plausible scenario: The marker genes might transfer in the human gut to other gut bacteria that would then be resistant to antibiotics. While there is a remote chance that this could happen, research has again shown that it is highly unlikely. Most DNA is rapidly digested in the mouth and stomach. Very few genes remain intact. Those that do survive digestion would have to compete for entry into bacteria with the large amount [of] DNA that humans ordinarily eat.

Finally, incorporation of a new gene into a bacterium is itself a rare event. If the new gene is inserted, the chance that it will function correctly is miniscule. Remember that many billions of bacteria in the soil and in the human gut already are resistant to the antibiotic marker that was used in the development of the new crop variety.

*What's the bottom line? Should I worry about antibiotic resistance in bioengineered plants?*

It bears repeating that scientists have tried unsuccessfully for years to demonstrate the transfer of marker genes from plants to bacteria. If it occurs in nature, it occurs at an undetectably low rate. This is consistent with the observation that biotech crops containing antibiotic resistance genes have been planted for 12 years [as of 2008] on over a billion acres with no observable effect on the incidence of resistance to the antibiotic against which they are resistant.

If you must, worry about antibiotic-resistant infections from hospitals and clinical medical practice. The misuse and overuse of antibiotics in humans, animals and agriculture are the major factors that contribute to the rise of antibiotic resistance. As mentioned earlier, antibiotic resistance genes are already widespread. As consumers, each of us needs to insure that antibiotics are taken at the prescribed dosage for the recommended period of time.

> *"The unrestricted use of antibiotics in aquaculture . . . has the potential to affect human and animal health on a global scale."*

# Antibiotic Use in Aquaculture Is Excessive and Dangerous

*Felipe C. Cabello*

*Felipe C. Cabello is a professor of microbiology and immunology at New York Medical College. In the following viewpoint, he states that antibiotics are widely used in industrial fish farming, or aquaculture. He argues that evidence suggests that the use of antibiotics has created resistant bacterial strains in fish and that these resistant bacteria have transferred their resistance to bacteria strains found in humans. He argues that dangerous antibiotic-resistant bacteria may develop as a result of antibiotic use in aquaculture. Therefore, he concludes that antibiotic use in aquaculture should be much reduced.*

As you read, consider the following questions:

1. What hygienic shortcomings in the raising of fish does Cabello mention?

Felipe C. Cabello, "Heavy Use of Prophylactic Antibiotics in Aquaculture: A Growing Problem for Human and Animal Health and for the Environment," *Environmental Microbiology*, 2006, pp. 1137–1144. Copyright © 2006 The Author. Journal compilation copyright © 2006 Society for Applied Microbiology and Blackwell Publishing Ltd. Reproduced by permission of Blackwell Publishers.

2. What countries does Cabello give as examples of places where antibiotic use in aquaculture has not been restricted?

3. How long does Cabello say it took after industrial aquaculture began for evidence of the transfer of antibiotic resistance from animal to human bacteria? Was this slower or faster than it took for such transfers to occur as a result of land-based farming?

Industrial aquaculture [fish farming] is a rapidly growing industry in many developed and developing countries. It is expected that this growth will increase at an even faster rate in the future, stimulated by the depletion of fisheries and the market forces that globalize the sources of food supply. The last 20 years have seen a fourfold growth in industrial aquaculture worldwide. This impressive industrial development has been accompanied by some practices potentially damaging to human and animal health that include passing large amounts of veterinary drugs into the environment. For example, the aquaculture of shrimp and salmon has been accompanied by an important use of prophylactic [preventative] antibiotics in the aquatic environment of rivers, lakes and oceans. As expected, and as has occurred in other industrial settings or animal husbandry, this use has resulted in an increased antibiotic resistance of bacteria in the environment. Moreover, this development has been accompanied by an increase of antibiotic resistance in fish pathogens. The emergence of antibiotic resistance among fish pathogens undermines the effectiveness of the prophylactic use of antibiotics in aquaculture and increases the possibilities for passage not only of these antibiotic-resistant bacteria but also of their antibiotic resistance determinants to bacteria of terrestrial animals and human beings, including pathogens.

## Antibiotic Use in Aquaculture

In the aquaculture of fish, especially that of salmon and trout, nearly all manipulations undergone by the fish as they are being raised are stressors [that is, farming the fish puts stress on their systems]. Because these manipulations decrease the effectiveness of the fish's immune system to clear up bacterial colonization and infection, it has become common to increase the use of prophylactic antibiotics. Moreover, hygienic shortcomings in fish-raising methods, including increased fish population densities, crowding of farming sites in coastal waters, lack of sanitary barriers and failure to isolate fish farming units with infected animals, have increased the possibility of rapid spread of infections. This scenario also results in an augmented use of prophylactic antibiotics, often with the misplaced goal of forestalling these sanitary shortcomings. Fish are given antibiotics as a component of their food, and occasionally in baths and injections. The unconsumed food, and fish faeces, containing antibiotics reach the sediment at the bottom of the raising pens; antibiotics are leached from the food and faeces and diffuse into the sediment and they can be washed by currents to distant sites. Once in the environment, these antibiotics can be ingested by wild fish and other organisms including shellfish. These residual antibiotics will remain in the sediment, exerting selective pressure, thereby altering the composition of the microflora [tiny plants] of the sediment and selecting for antibiotic-resistant bacteria. There are a number of important studies that indicate that the bacterial flora in the environment surrounding aquaculture sites contain an increased number of antibiotic-resistant bacteria, and that these bacteria harbour new and previously uncharacterized resistance determinants [genetic abilities to resist antibiotics]. The determinants of antibiotic resistance that have emerged and selected in this aquatic environment have the potential of being transmitted by horizontal gene transfer to bacteria of the terrestrial environment, including human and

## Antibiotics in Chilean Aquaculture

In 2005, the OECD (Organisation for Economic Co-operation and Development) released a report with strong criticism of the Chilean salmon industry, given the escape of one million fish each year, the use of fungicides such as malachite green—a carcinogen—and the excessive use of antibiotics that has been prohibited since 2002. Doctor [Felipe] Cabello estimated that Chile uses between 70 and 300 times more antibiotics than Norway, and there is a black market for salmon antibiotics in the country.

*Raúl Zibechi, "Consequences of the 'Chilean Miracle,'" Panama News, vol. 15, no. 15, September 4, 2009.*

animal pathogens. The exchange of resistance determinants between the aquatic and terrestrial environment can also stem from the movement of antibiotic-resistant bacteria between these two environments, a result of transporting fish between bodies of freshwater and the ocean. . . . In many aquaculture settings in developing countries, the possibilities of these exchanges have been amplified by the high level of contamination of seawater and freshwater with untreated sewage and agricultural and industrial wastewater containing normal intestinal flora and pathogens of animals and humans usually resistant to antibiotics. . . .

## Fish Bacteria and Human Bacteria

Not unexpectedly, exchange of genes for resistance to antibiotics between bacteria in the aquaculture environment and bacteria in the terrestrial environment, including bacteria of animals and human pathogens has recently been shown. For example, strong epidemiological and molecular evidence exists indicating that fish pathogens such as *Aeromonas* can transmit and share determinants for resistance to antibiotics with pathogens such as *Escherichia coli* isolated from humans. . . .

Molecular and epidemiological evidence has demonstrated that antibiotic resistance determinants of resistant *Salmonella enterica* serotype Typhimurium DT104, an emergent pathogen and the cause of several outbreaks of salmonellosis [a dangerous illness] in humans and animals in Europe and the USA, probably originated in aquaculture settings of the Far East. . . .

The presence of antibiotics in the aquatic environment can result in the appearance of resistance among human pathogens. . . . For example, *V[ibrio] cholerae* of the Latin American epidemic of cholera that started in 1992 appeared to have acquired antibiotic resistance as a result of coming into contact with antibiotic-resistant bacteria selected through the heavy use of antibiotics in the Ecuadorian shrimp industry. . . . Thus, the commonality of antibiotic resistance determinants and of genetic elements between aquatic bacteria, fish pathogens and bacteria from the terrestrial environment strongly supports the concept that antibiotic usage in aquaculture will influence the appearance of resistance in bacteria of other niches, including resistance in pathogens able to produce a variety of human and animal diseases. . . .

Another problem created by the excessive use of antibiotics in industrial aquaculture is the presence of residual antibiotics in commercialized and shellfish products. This problem has led to undetected consumption of antibiotics by consumers of fish with the added potential alteration of their normal flora that increases their susceptibility to bacterial infections and also selects for antibiotic-resistant bacteria. Moreover, undetected consumption of antibiotics in food can generate problems of allergy and toxicity, which are difficult to diagnose because of a lack of previous information on antibiotic ingestion. Allergy to antibiotics and problems of toxicity can also be created for the unprotected workers in the aquaculture industry through the use of large amounts of antibiotics that come in contact with the skin and intestinal and bronchial tracts as workers medicate the food in food mills, distribute it, and administer it to fish. In aquaculture, the passage into and permanent existence of large amounts of antibiotics in the environment of water and sediments also have the potential to affect the presence of the normal flora and plankton in those niches, resulting in shifts in the diversity of the microbiota [microscopic life]. . . . As the microbiota carries important trophic [nutritional] and metabolic functions in aquatic and sediment niches, this heavy use [of] antibiotics also has the potential to alter the ecological equilibria at those levels, thus creating situations that may impact fish and human health by promoting, for example, algal blooms [the rapid increase of algae] and anoxic environments [environments with low oxygen].

## Restrictions on Antibiotics

Evidence indicating that antibiotic-resistant bacteria and antibiotic resistance determinants pass from the aquatic to the terrestrial environment has resulted in a drastic restriction of the use of antibiotics in aquaculture in many countries. Restrictions have included increased control of the prescription of therapeutic antibiotics, almost total elimination of the use of antibiotic prophylaxis in this setting and proscription of the use of antibiotics in therapeutics that are still very useful in the therapy of human infections. In this way, the use of quinolones [a kind of antibiotic] has been totally restricted in aquaculture in industrialized countries, not only because they are a highly effective group of antibiotics for human infections but also because of their ability to generate cross-resistance among all the members of this group. Quinolones also remain active in sediments for prolonged periods of time as they are not readily biodegradable [that is, they do not decompose easily]. This increased control of antibiotic use, accompanied by sanitary measures that include the use of vaccines, have drastically reduced the use of antibiotics in the aquaculture industry of developed countries, therefore indicating that it is economically feasible to develop a productive aquaculture industry without excessive prophylactic use of antibiotics. However, the use of quinolones and many other antibiotics remains totally unrestricted in aquaculture in countries with growing aquaculture industries such as China and Chile. For example, in Chile, statistics indicate that annually 10–12 metric tons of quinolones are used in human medicine and approximately 100–110 metric tons of these antibiotics are used in veterinary medicine per year, most of them in aquaculture. In this country the use of flumequine, a fluoroquinolone used exclusively in aquaculture, has increased from approximately 30 metric tons in 1998 to close to 100 metric tons in 2002. This increase in the use of this broad-spectrum [useful against many kinds of bacteria] fluoroquinolone parallels the increase in the production of salmon from 258,000 metric tons in 1998 to 494,000 metric tons in 2002. This suggests that in Chile, aquaculture use of quinolones and not human use will probably be the most important selective pressure to generate the emergence of quinolone-resistant bacteria. Similarly in China, quinolone resistance has emerged as an important public health problem as [a] result of the unrestricted use of this group of antibiotics in aquaculture and in industrial animal husbandry. . . .

## A Global Threat

This brief review suggests that the unrestricted use of antibiotics in aquaculture in any country has the potential to affect human and animal health on a global scale, and further suggests that this problem should be dealt through unified local and global preventive approaches. The use of antibiotics in aquaculture shares characteristics with a heavy use of antibiotics in alternative industrial processes of animal husbandry. It, nonetheless, has specific characteristics. It would appear that the transfer of antibiotic resistance determinants among bacteria of the aquatic and terrestrial environment would be readily attained, simply as a result of the high concentrations of bacteria in seawater and aquatic sediments and the abundant presence of bacteriophages to facilitate such a transfer. Contamination of the bodies of water where aquaculture is practised with bacteria of the normal flora and pathogens of the intestine of humans and animals will also accelerate this transfer. Approximately 20 years after industrial aquaculture had begun, evidence emerged of the transfer of antibiotic resistance determinants between aquatic bacteria, including fish pathogens and human pathogens. Historical evidence appears to indicate that in terrestrial animal husbandry this process took a longer time. The acceleration of this process strongly suggests that heavy antibiotic use in aquaculture needs to be reduced drastically and replaced with improved sanitation in fish husbandry to avoid the emergence of antibiotic resistance in fish pathogens and environmental bacteria and the passing of this resistance to human pathogens, thus endangering effective therapy to treat human bacterial infections. Experience with alternative processes of animal husbandry and aquaculture itself indicates that these much-needed changes to protect human and animal health can be achieved without detrimental effects, in financial terms, to the industry.

# Periodical Bibliography

*The following articles have been selected to supplement the diverse views presented in this chapter.*

Associated Press "Growing Pressure to Stop Antibiotics in Agriculture," *Drug Discovery & Development*, January 4, 2010. www.dddmag.com.

Katie Couric "Animal Antibiotic Overuse Hurting Humans?" *CBS Evening News*, February 9, 2010. www.cbs news.com.

European Food Safety Authority "EFSA Evaluates Antibiotic Resistance Marker Genes in GM Plants," June 11, 2009. www.efsa .europa.eu.

H. Scott Hurd and Tracy Ann Raef "ISU Associate Professor and Former USDA Deputy Undersecretary Food Safety Responds to CBS News Segments on Antibiotics - Feb. 9 and 10," Iowa State University College of Veterinary Medicine, February 10, 2010. http://vet med.iastate.edu.

Sue Jarrett and David Wallinga "Dangers of Agricultural Antibiotics," *Denver Post*, January 16, 2007. www.denverpost.com.

Alyn M. McClure "Opinions/Editorials: Animal Agriculture and Responsible Antibiotic Use," Arizona Farm Bureau, February 10, 2010. www.azfb.org.

Pilar Hernández Serrano *Responsible Use of Antibiotics in Aquaculture* (FAO Fisheries Technical Paper No. 469), Food and Agriculture Organization of the United Nations, 2005. www.fao.org.

Rod Smith "Antibiotics Called 'Vital Tool,'" Feedstuffs FoodLink, October 2, 2008. www.feedstuffs foodlink.com.

OPPOSING
VIEWPOINTS®
SERIES

CHAPTER 3

# How Should Antibiotics Be Used to Combat Different Diseases?

# Chapter Preface

A ntibiotics are used to treat a number of conditions other than standard bacterial infections. One of their most common uses is in the treatment of acne.

Acne occurs when "hair follicles become plugged with oil and dead skin cells," according to MayoClinic.com. The plugged follicle can become infected, causing a raised red spot called a pimple. Infections or blockages beneath the skin can also produce lumps called cysts or cystic acne.

Antibiotics can help reduce acne in several ways. "The most important is the decrease in the number of bacteria in and around the follicle," according to Heather Brannon in a December 7, 2009, article. Antibiotics also cut down on chemicals produced by white blood cells that can cause acne.

For acne, physicians may prescribe topical antibiotic creams such as clindamycin or erythromycin. It is also common to prescribe oral antibiotics, including erythromycin or tetracycline. The article "Prescription Medications for Treating Acne" on AcneNet explains, "For patients with moderate to severe and persistent acne, oral antibiotics have been a mainstay of therapy for years." The article adds that antibiotics are usually prescribed for a maximum of six months. Brannon notes that antibiotic use can result in vaginal infections in girls. Other side effects, according to MayoClinic.com, may include "upset stomach, dizziness or skin discoloration. These drugs also increase your skin's sun sensitivity and may also reduce the effectiveness of oral contraceptives."

One concern with the prescription of antibiotics for acne is the possible increase in antibiotic resistance. The AcneNet article discussed earlier states that, over time, the bacteria that cause acne may become "resistant to the antibiotic being used to treat it," requiring a switch to a new treatment. Another worry is that the treatment may make users more susceptible to infection. David Margolis, one of the authors of a study on the effect of long-term antibiotic use for acne, said that acne sufferers treated with antibiotics "were about twice as likely to develop an upper respiratory tract infection within a year's period of time" (as quoted in a January 19, 2006, article by Allison Aubrey on *NPR Online*). The study did not show that antibiotics were causing the increased number of infections; nonetheless, doctors have begun to try to reduce dosages of antibiotics for acne sufferers in an effort to reduce risks.

The viewpoints in this chapter will look at the effectiveness and safety of treating other conditions with antibiotics.

> *"Within 12 hours Mom's horribly swollen feet shrank down to normal size, arch and all. . . . She was practically dancing, so grateful to the miracle of penicillin!"*

# Antibiotics Should Be Used to Treat Arthritis

*Rima Kittley*

*Rima Kittley is a board-certified family medicine physician and an herbalist with a practice in Lufkin, Texas. In the following viewpoint, she explains that she used antibiotics to treat her mother's rheumatoid arthritis and that the effectiveness of the therapy convinced her that antibiotics can cure arthritis and other autoimmune conditions. Kittley states that she has used antibiotics to treat a range of autoimmune illnesses during her years of practice.*

As you read, consider the following questions:

1. Why did Kittley choose penicillin as the first antibiotic with which to treat her mother?
2. Why did Kittley switch to using Rocephin?

3. What people does Kittley say are likely to have strep-caused arthritis?

Medical internship. A time for 90-hour workweeks. A time for putting into practice all my medical school book-learning. A time for no sleep. And a time for phone calls from Mom. "What do I do about this?" "What does it mean when Grandma has that?" And then the fateful call: "My Kaiser doctor says I have rheumatoid arthritis. . . . He tells me to get a wheelchair to save my feet. . . . You've got to find something to help me!"

## A Miracle with Penicillin

She honestly believed I could find the answer the medical profession could not. Long story short, Mom found it for me. At the time, I only knew what I was taught in medical school: Rheumatoid arthritis is an autoimmune disease [a disease caused by the body's immune system attacking itself], and we don't know what causes or cures it. This answer was unacceptable to her. It meant ending up a cripple the rest of her life.

Understand, I was the third generation of women in my family to head into a medical career. My grandmother went to medical school for three years before being nudged out by my grandfather. My mother was accepted, but never went, because I came along. She taught high school sciences instead. So when I was accepted and then actually made it all the way through to an MD [Doctor of Medicine], it was a big deal! Internship was not exactly the best time to ask me to solve what seemed unsolvable. The blank stares she got from me were certainly from lack of sleep instead of wheels grinding in my brain. "Mom, I can't even write a prescription on my own yet," I would say. Needless to say, I wasn't much help. So she went on her own quest.

Mom's quest was not how I would have done it. She spent hours and hours trying to come up with *WHY* this was all happening to her. She didn't care what others believed about it. She didn't have years of medical school brainwashing to sift through. As my internship year rolled into the second year of family practice residency, Mom could hardly walk. This was about the time news came out that some arthritis was caused by an infection called Lyme disease [an infection often caused by tick bites]. Mom worked and worked on me to treat her "Lyme disease." I was not about to budge. "No," I said. "I don't know what I'm treating. And you never had a tick bite."

One day after a very long call weekend, she pulled rank on me. "I'm your mother! Give me antibiotics!!" Oh, my. I just lost the battle of wits. Sigh. Let's see, what did I learn in medical school? Lyme disease is a spirochete, sort of like syphilis [a sexually transmitted bacterial infection]. Penicillin works for syphilis. Penicillin couldn't hurt, was my thought, and it would get Mom off my back. It certainly is more benign than steroids and the other drugs rheumatologists use.

What happened next was absolutely incredible. Within 12 hours Mom's horribly swollen feet shrank down to normal size, arch and all. Her pain was gone for the first time in months. She was practically dancing, so grateful to the miracle of penicillin!

By the end of a week, the miracle faded. The pain and swelling returned. Of course, Mom wanted the miracle back, so she insisted on another shot of penicillin. I wanted to see if this was real or just a fluke. OK. More penicillin. Same thing happened again. The pain and swelling disappeared. We repeated this miracle four times. Each time, the beneficial effects of the penicillin faded more quickly.

## Not a Coincidence

It could not have been a coincidence, I thought. I had to concede Mom was on to something, but penicillin wasn't quite the right medicine. I scrambled to find out more about Lyme disease myself. Very little was written about it since this was all new information. I ended up calling Lyme disease researchers in Minnesota and New York. Rocephin intravenously, I was told, was a much better choice for treating Lyme disease than penicillin. Mom's lab work came back "negative" for Lyme disease, but by this time I didn't care. Antibiotics were really helping her. We proceeded with 14 days of IV [intravenous] Rocephin therapy in the living room.

Seeing was believing . . . maybe. Mom improved enough to return to work. She went back to Kaiser to show them how much better she was. Her doctor insisted that rheumatoid arthritis doesn't get better, and she had been misdiagnosed. He also told her she couldn't have had Lyme disease, and referred her to a psychiatrist. I was never particularly convinced she had Lyme disease either, but something certainly responded to antibiotic therapy.

With the busyness of medical training, the memory of Mom's dramatic penicillin therapy faded. So did my belief in antibiotics. Mom's joint problems were better and worse, though never to the severity of that summer. Mom continued her vigilance for other arthritis treatments. She happened to have her TV on *Good Morning America* when [the late] Dr. Thomas McPherson Brown spoke about treating arthritis with antibiotics. I got a phone call, "Quick! Turn on the TV! There's a doctor talking about treating arthritis with antibiotics." "Sure, Mom, you watch. I can't get to the TV right now." Years later, I was sorry I missed it.

Mom hounded, and I mean hounded, me to keep her in antibiotics. She wrote to Dr. Brown's foundation and brought me as much information as she could get her hands on, including the book *The Road Back*. I got every article she came across shoved in front of me with an oral quiz at the end. Then, of course, she would refer arthritic patients to me, telling them her story. Early in my practice, I dared to treat only a select few with antibiotics. It probably took 10 years for me to truly believe in what I was doing. It became easier after the

*JAMA* [the *Journal of the American Medical Association*] study about Minocin validated antibiotic therapy for arthritis.

During my 14 years of practice, I have treated all kinds of rheumatoid diseases including scleroderma, lupus, chronic Lyme disease, rheumatoid arthritis and fibromyalgia. Sometimes the results are absolutely awe-inspiring. Sometimes people do not have the patience to continue therapy until they get better.

As a family physician, I tend to look at the whole person and ask a lot of history questions before embarking on antibiotic therapy, if it is appropriate. I don't have an exact protocol. I know the various antibiotics well, and I'm not afraid to use them. I will treat with IV antibiotics or shots or oral medications depending on the circumstances. There are many more antibiotics available now than there were in Dr. Brown's time, so why not use them? Most of what works has to be determined clinically anyway, since lab tests are not particularly helpful.

## Rethinking Illnesses

The hardest part is rethinking the illness patterns. Is there really such a thing as autoimmune disease? Maybe it's all triggered by infection. And each person is different. For example, someone who had recurrent and severe strep infections as a child, I think, is likely to have strep-caused arthritis, whether or not the ASO titers [a blood test for strep infections] are elevated. I will more likely treat them with amoxicillin or Zithromax or Biaxin that hits the strep-type bugs hard. The tetracyclines don't work as well on strep-type infections.

The next hardest part is realizing that the patterns may be more than one disease. People can and do have two or three infections going on at the same time. Or two or three disease processes. Time and patience and listening to the patient provide an answer. Blast the obvious infections first, like chronic

## Rheumatoid Arthritis and Scleroderma Patients Compare Antibiotic Therapy to Traditional Drug Therapy

| Which Treatment Was Effective At: | Percentage of Patients Who Said Antibiotic Treatment | Percentage of Patients Who Said Traditional Medication |
| --- | --- | --- |
| Slowing progress of disease | 92% | 39% |
| Decreasing levels of pain | 91% | 64% |
| Reducing stiffness | 92% | 58% |
| Reducing swelling | 89% | 58% |
| Improving quality of life | 94% | 54% |
| Increasing ability to function at home | 94% | 57% |
| Reducing fatigue | 93% | 38% |

TAKEN FROM: *Road Back Foundation Website,* "New Survey Reveals Common Low-Cost Antibiotic Therapy May Have Considerable Benefits for Rheumatoid Arthritis Patients, Reports Road Back Foundation," February 15, 2006.

sinusitis or chronic kidney infections, with heavy-duty antibiotics. Then back off and treat the chronic indolent ones with less potent drugs. I did this with a scleroderma [an autoimmune disease] patient once. I blasted her with IV Rocephin for her sinusitis and her scleroderma remarkably improved. If a particular antibiotic does not work after a few months, I try a different one. Minocin that is supposed to be the best for tissue penetration does not work for some. I probably use the tetracycline-type antibiotics the most for long-term therapy. I wish I had an answer as to why the body does not fight these infections off permanently.

By the way, Mom is doing just fine, thanks. She gets around and does most everything she wants to. She has been on mostly tetracycline for the last 13 years. I take tetracycline for my own fibromyalgia-type arthritis. I am, after all, my mother's daughter. Hurray for persistent mothers!

*"Their findings suggest that doxycycline may slow the progression of joint damage and point to the need for further research into the drug's effect on the signs and symptoms of this disease."*

# More Research Is Needed into the Use of Antibiotics to Treat Arthritis

## Health & Medicine Week

*Health & Medicine Week is a newsletter for NewsRX, the world's largest source for health information. In the following viewpoint, the authors note a study that has shown that the antibiotic doxycycline can benefit those with osteoarthritis (OA). Although the testing suggested that the antibiotic may slow the progression of joint damage, further studies are necessary to determine the effect the drug could have on the symptoms of the disease.*

As you read, consider the following questions:

1. What is osteoarthritis (OA)?
2. During the trial, how often was the severity of joint pain assessed?

*Health & Medicine Week*, "Tetracycline Antibiotic Successfully Treats OA," July 18, 2005. Reproduced by permission.

3. What were some unexpected benefits of the antibiotic that some participants experienced during the trial period?

Doxycycline has been successfully used to treat a wide range of bacterial infections. In addition to its effects as an antibiotic, doxycycline has other actions as a drug and in laboratory studies with animals and with human tissue, it was shown to inhibit the degradation of cartilage in a way that could be useful for the treatment of osteoarthritis (OA).

OA is a common form of arthritis associated with pain and disability related to the breakdown of cartilage, the tissue in the joint that absorbs shock and promotes smooth movement.

On the strength of preclinical evidence, a team of rheumatologists affiliated with six clinical research centers across the United States conducted the first long-term clinical trial to determine the benefits of doxycycline in the treatment of OA—particularly OA of the knee. Their findings suggest that doxycycline may slow the progression of joint damage and point to the need for further research into the drug's effect on the signs and symptoms of this disease.

## Antibiotic Trial

For the trial, the team recruited 431 overweight women between the ages of 45 and 64 with moderately advanced OA in one knee. The subjects were randomly assigned to receive either 100 milligrams of doxycycline or a placebo twice a day for 30 months. At baseline, the two treatment groups were roughly equal with respect to all demographic variables, body mass index, and types of drugs taken for pain, as well as for the X-ray severity of OA in the affected knee and the level of knee pain and functional impairment.

OA progression was assessed by measuring joint space narrowing in the medial tibiofemoral compartment through

X-rays obtained at baseline, 16 months and 30 months. Severity of joint pain was assessed every six months after a washout period of all nonsteroidal anti-inflammatory drugs (NSAIDs) and analgesics.

Seventy-one percent of the subjects completed the treatment protocol. Radiographs were obtained from 85% of all subjects at 30 months. After 16 months of treatment, the mean loss of joint space width in the diseased knee in the doxycycline group was 40% less than in the placebo group. After 30 months, it was 33% less.

Yet, despite significantly slowing disease progression, doxycycline did not reduce the severity of joint pain. However, mean pain scores at baseline were low in both treatment groups, leaving only limited opportunity to demonstrate improvement in joint pain. On the other hand, the drug significantly reduced the frequency with which subjects reported increases in knee pain 20 percent or greater than the level of pain they had at their previous semi-annual visit.

Notably, doxycycline seemed to have no effect on joint space narrowing or pain in the relatively disease-free knee. In both knees in both treatment groups, the rate of joint space narrowing was more than twice as rapid in subjects who reported frequent increases in pain than in those with a stable pain score. "Joint pain may serve as an indicator of synovitis that leads to cartilage destruction," observed the study's leading author, Kenneth D. Brandt, MD.

## Study Conclusions

Throughout the trial, fewer than 5% of all subjects reported side effects. In general, doxycycline seemed to be well tolerated. Subjects in the active treatment group experienced the unexpected side benefits of fewer urinary tract and upper respiratory tract infections than their placebo counterparts.

In conclusion, in this study, doxycycline showed benefits in slowing the rate of joint space narrowing in knees with established OA. Whether this drug has any value in the early treatment and symptomatic management of OA, however, will require further investigation.

> *"Prolonged antibiotic therapy appears to be useful and justifiable in chronic Lyme disease."*

# Long-Term Antibiotic Therapy May Be Useful in Treating Lyme Disease

*Raphael B. Stricker*

*Raphael B. Stricker is the medical director of Union Square Medical Associates in San Francisco. In the following viewpoint, he argues that the bacteria responsible for Lyme disease are very adaptable and complex. He also argues that Lyme disease is a difficult illness to treat and that evidence suggests that initial treatment with antibiotics is not always successful. He states that some research has shown success with longer-term treatment with antibiotics and concludes that longer-term antibiotic treatment for Lyme disease is sometimes justified.*

As you read, consider the following questions:

1. How many gene sequences with how many functioning genes does Stricker say *B. burgdorferi* has?

Raphael B. Stricker, "Counterpoint: Long-Term Antibiotic Therapy Improves Persistent Symptoms Associated with Lyme Disease," *Clinical Infectious Diseases*, June 5, 2007, pp. 149–157. Copyright © 2007 by the Infectious Diseases Society of America. All rights reserved. Reproduced by permission.

2. After two to four weeks of antibiotic therapy, what percentage of patients have been noted to have persistent symptoms, according to Stricker?

3. What is *Babesia*, and how might it complicate Lyme disease?

L yme disease is a controversial illness. The classic features of the disease include receipt of a tick bite followed by the so called erythema migrans or "bull's-eye" rash and significant joint swelling typical of arthritis. Unfortunately, the classic features of this tick-borne disease are not always present. For example, only 50%–60% of patients with Lyme disease recall having received a tick bite, and often the erythema migrans rash is absent or not in the shape of a bull's-eye. According to health departments around the United States, the typical bull's-eye rash is only reported in 35%–60% of patients with Lyme disease. Furthermore, frank arthritis is only seen in 20%–30% of patients with Lyme disease. Thus, the classic features of the disease may be absent, and the diagnosis may be easily missed.

## Lyme Disease Is Hard to Detect

In the absence of typical features of Lyme disease, patients may go on to develop a syndrome with multiple nonspecific symptoms that affect various organ systems, including the joints, muscles, nerves, brain, and heart. The myriad symptoms prompt the question whether this is "post-Lyme disease syndrome," a poorly defined entity triggered by Lyme disease, or whether these symptoms are caused by persistent infection with the Lyme spirochete [a kind of bacteria], *Borrelia burgdorferi*. To address this question, we must first examine the pathophysiology [biological changes caused as a result] of the disease.

*B. burgdorferi* is a fascinating bacterium. It has [more than] 1500 gene sequences with at least 132 functioning genes.

In contrast, *Treponema pallidum*, the spirochetal agent of syphilis [a dangerous sexually transmitted disease], has only 22 functioning genes. The genetic makeup of *B. burgdorferi* is quite unusual. It has a linear chromosome and 21 plasmids, which are extrachromosomal strands of DNA. This is 3 times more plasmids than any other known bacteria (*Chlamydia* comes in a distant second, with 7 plasmids). Plasmids are thought to give bacteria a kind of "rapid response" system that allows them to adapt very rapidly to changes in the environment, and the complex genetic structure of *B. burgdorferi* suggests that this is a highly adaptable organism. . . .

Let's turn briefly to laboratory testing in Lyme disease. A major problem is that current commercial Lyme . . . tests are not sensitive enough for diagnosis, especially during the later stages of disease. . . .

Thus, the diagnosis of Lyme disease remains problematic, with as many as one-half of patients experiencing failure with the current . . . testing approach.

## Treatment of Lyme Disease

With this background concerning the clinical diagnostic problems, complex pathophysiology, and testing difficulties related to *B. burgdorferi*, we arrive at the topic of this debate, which is treatment failure in Lyme disease. Documented treatment failure with culture-confirmed *B. burgdorferi* infection was first reported [more than] 17 years ago [in 1990], so it was surprising to see a quotation in the *New York Times* by 2 members of the Infectious Diseases Society of America (IDSA) Lyme disease guidelines committee stating that "[there] is no credible scientific evidence for the persistence of symptomatic *B. burgdorferi* infection after antibiotic treatment." Let's review the "credible scientific evidence" for persistence of this infection taken from articles published over the past 17 years.

## Diseases Besides Lyme Disease That Require Prolonged Antibiotic Therapy

| Disease | Organism | Treatment | Duration of Treatment, Months |
| --- | --- | --- | --- |
| Drug-susceptible tuberculosis | Mycobacterium tuberculosis | 2–4 antibiotics | 6–9 |
| Multidrug-resistant tuberculosis | M. tuberculosis | 3–5 antibiotics | 18–24 |
| Leprosy | Mycobacterium leprae | 3–4 antibiotics | 24 |
| Atypical tuberculosis | Mycobacterium chelonae | Oral and intravenous antibiotics | 6–12 |
| Q fever endocarditis | Coxiella burnetii | 2 antibiotics | 36 |

TAKEN FROM: Raphael B. Stricker, "Counterpoint: Long-Term Antibiotic Therapy Improves Persistent Symptoms Associated with Lyme Disease," *Clinical Infectious Diseases*, June 5, 2007, 45, p. 153.

We can start with animal models of Lyme disease. In the mouse, one study found that . . . "nine months after treatment, low levels of spirochete DNA could be detected . . . in a subset of antibiotic treated mice." So at least in the mouse model, spirochetes may persist after appropriate treatment.

Next is the dog model—a particularly convincing model, because . . . in dogs that had been experimentally infected with *B. burgdorferi* by tick exposure, treatment with high doses of amoxicillin or doxycycline for 30 days diminished persistent infection but failed to eliminate it. Furthermore, when dogs were observed for a 500-day postinfection period (the equivalent of 3–4 human years), *B. burgdorferi* DNA was detectable at low levels in multiple tissue samples obtained from the dogs, despite the administration of "adequate" antibiotic treatment. . . .

In summary, these animal models provide "credible scientific evidence" for persistent infection in Lyme disease.

Turning to human studies, there are a number of reports that show persistent symptoms of Lyme disease after short-term antibiotic therapy. Persistent symptoms have been noted in 25%–80% of patients with Lyme disease after 2–4 weeks of antibiotic therapy. Furthermore, infection that was determined to be persistent . . . has been documented in up to 40% of patients following receipt of the "adequate" antibiotic treatment recommended by the IDSA. . . . These reports suggest that short-term antibiotic therapy may suppress the Lyme spirochete but not eradicate it.

In another case, the patient's condition deteriorated despite receipt of repeated courses of antibiotic treatment over a 2-year period. She received 12 months of intravenous antibiotic treatment, followed by 11 months of oral antibiotics, and her condition improved significantly. Thus, this case report suggests that longer treatment may be beneficial in some patients with Lyme disease. Taken as a whole, these studies provide "credible scientific evidence" for persistence of *B. burg-*

*dorferi* infection after "adequate" short-term antibiotic treatment in humans.

## Will Longer Treatment Help?

That brings up the next question: Does longer antibiotic treatment help in persistent Lyme disease? There have been a number of uncontrolled trials that support longer treatment of persistent disease symptoms. The largest study included 277 patients who were treated with tetracycline for 1–11 months (mean duration, 4 months). The study showed that, after 2 months of therapy, 33% of patients had improvement in symptoms, but after 3 months of treatment, 61% of patients had decreased symptoms. So this study suggests that longer treatment may result in better symptom outcome in Lyme disease. There have been other small, uncontrolled trials showing that longer treatment may have better symptom outcomes in patients with Lyme disease, including one trial that showed that patients who were re-treated with intravenous therapy had the greatest improvement in their symptoms.

In addition to infection with *B. burgdorferi*, tick-borne coinfections are being recognized more frequently. If a patient is treated for Lyme disease and has symptoms that have persisted or worsened, the lack of improvement may be due to the presence of *Babesia, Anaplasma, Ehrlichia, or Bartonella* coinfection [the patient may have been infected with other bacteria at the same time he or she was infected with Lyme disease]. Coinfection with *Babesia* and *Ehrlichia* has been shown to exacerbate Lyme disease in mouse models and also in humans. . . . *Babesia, Anaplasma, Ehrlichia* and *Bartonella* . . . may cause low-grade infections that can increase the severity and duration of Lyme disease. . . .

What is the approach for a patient who presents with persistent symptoms of Lyme disease? . . .

Coinfections should be treated first, if any are present, and then oral or parenteral [injected] antibiotics should be used to treat symptoms of persistent Lyme disease. Antibiotic therapy should be administered in a rotating and open-ended manner. . . .

This approach differs from the recommendations of the current IDSA guidelines, which do not recognize persistent infection in chronic Lyme disease. However, the treatment approach is consistent with the guidelines of the International Lyme and Associated Diseases Society, which mandates treatment for persistent infection in patients with chronic Lyme disease symptoms. . . . On the basis of the foregoing discussion, prolonged antibiotic therapy appears to be useful and justifiable in chronic Lyme disease.

In summary, [more than] 18,000 scientific articles have been written about Lyme disease. Some of these articles focus on the complex pathophysiology of *B. burgdorferi*, whereas others highlight the clinical uncertainty surrounding tick-borne disease. Because the optimal therapy for this complicated illness is still in doubt, we must keep an open mind about the treatment of patients who present with persistent symptoms of Lyme and associated tick-borne diseases.

"For most patients with a positive Lyme antibody titer and only symptoms of fatigue or nonspecific muscle pains, the risks and cost of intravenous antibiotic therapy exceed the benefits."

# Long-Term IV Antibiotics Are Overused in the Treatment of Lyme Disease

*Edward McSweegan*

*Edward McSweegan is a microbiologist who lives and works in Maryland. Between 1993 and 1995, he managed a federal Lyme disease research program. In the following viewpoint, McSweegan argues that Lyme disease is a bacterial infection that responds readily to antibiotic treatment. Despite the evidence, however, he says that many patients have convinced themselves that Lyme disease is a chronic illness that must be treated with long-term use of intravenous antibiotics and other extreme treatments. McSweegan argues that doctors who push such treatments are deceiving and endangering patients.*

As you read, consider the following questions:

1. What is the Lyme disease rash called and what does it look like?
2. What negative results can long-term intravenous antibiotic therapy have, according to McSweegan?
3. What is "herxing"?

L yme disease is the most common tick-borne disease in the United States. In 2006, the Centers for Disease Control and Prevention (CDC) recorded 17,002 cases. The infection is caused by *Borrelia burgdorferi*, a spiral-shaped bacterium (spirochete) named after Dr. Willy Burgdorfer, the public health researcher who discovered it in 1982. The infection is often contracted during warm-weather months when ticks are active. The spirochete enters the skin at the site of the tick bite. After incubating for 3–30 days, the bacteria migrate through the skin and may spread to lymph nodes or disseminate through the bloodstream to organs or distant skin sites.

## Controversies Around Lyme Disease

Lyme disease frequently presents with a skin rash called erythema migrans (EM) and common flu-like symptoms of fever, malaise, fatigue, and muscle and joint pains. The characteristic EM rash is a flat or raised red area that expands, often with clearing at the center, to a diameter of up to 20 inches. However, it does not always occur, which can make the diagnosis more difficult, especially when the patient is not aware of having been bitten by a tick. Other early signs may include small skin lesions, facial nerve paralysis, lymphocytic meningitis [an infection of membranes around the brain and spinal cord], and heart-rhythm disturbances. Early infections usually are cured by two to four weeks of orally administered antibiotics (amoxicillin or doxycycline). However, if untreated or inadequately treated, neurologic, cardiac, or joint abnormalities may follow. Worldwide, Lyme disease has been directly responsible for fewer than two dozen deaths.

The disease is named after the town of Old Lyme, Connecticut, where researchers recognized its nature in 1975. In Europe, associations between tick bites and several skin diseases had been known for decades, but it was not understood that various conditions were part of a single illness. Since its nature was clarified, Lyme disease has emerged as a significant source of public controversy. Some people claim to be persistently infected with *B. burgdorferi* and suffering from debilitating symptoms as a result.

Many infectious agents can cause chronic infections or can be difficult to eradicate with standard antibiotic treatments. Unfortunately, it is often difficult to diagnose such infections and, in the case of Lyme disease, it is difficult to know what percent of cases persist in the form of chronic infections. Other possibilities for persistent symptoms include: autoimmune-like reactions in which the body attacks its own organs and tissues; physically damaged or scarred organs and tissues from an earlier infection; another tick-borne infection such as babesiosis or ehrlichiosis; and re-infection by *B. burgdorferi*.

Of course, symptoms occurring long after the onset of Lyme disease also can be coincidental. A long-term study of 212 Connecticut residents suspected of having Lyme disease found incidences of pain, fatigue, and difficulty with daily activities to be similar to 212 age-matched controls without Lyme disease. As noted in an accompanying editorial:

> After a median follow-up of 51 months, patients with a diagnosis of Lyme disease that met the national surveillance case definition developed by the Centers for Disease Control and Prevention (CDC) had the same profile of symptoms and the same quality-of-life indicators as age-matched controls without Lyme disease. Thus, recognition and treatment of clear-cut Lyme disease resulted in a return to baseline

with no measurable sequelae [aftereffects]. On the other hand, patients who were reported to have Lyme disease but who did not meet the CDC's case definition of Lyme disease had increased symptoms and worsening quality-of-life indicators. The implication is that many of these individuals really did not have Lyme disease and therefore did not respond to the treatment.

## Limitations of Laboratory Tests

The diagnosis of Lyme disease should be based primarily on an evaluation of a patient's symptoms and the probability of exposure to the Lyme spirochete. Laboratory evaluation is appropriate for patients who have arthritic, neurologic, or cardiac symptoms associated with Lyme disease, but it is not warranted in patients who have nonspecific symptoms, such as those of chronic fatigue syndrome or fibromyalgia.

Matthew J. Rusk, MD, and Stephen J. Gluckman, MD, of the University of Pennsylvania summarized the diagnostic situation, noting that ". . . positive results do not prove that [the] patient has Lyme disease and have little predictive value in the absence of characteristic symptoms."

The FDA [U.S. Food and Drug Administration] agreed and outlined a two-step algorithm for laboratory testing. In a 1997 FDA Public Health Advisory, it advised physicians that:

> "The results of commonly marketed assays for detecting antibody to *Borrelia burgdorferi* (anti-Bb) . . . may be easily misinterpreted. . . . Although package inserts for some commercial assays describe their intended use 'to aid in the diagnosis of Lyme disease,' this statement does not fully reflect current knowledge . . . and many such assays yield potentially misleading results. . . . Assays for anti-Bb frequently yield false-positive results because of cross-reactive anti bodies associated with autoimmune diseases or from infection with other spirochetes, rickettsia, ehrlichia, or other bacteria such as *Helicobacter pylori*."

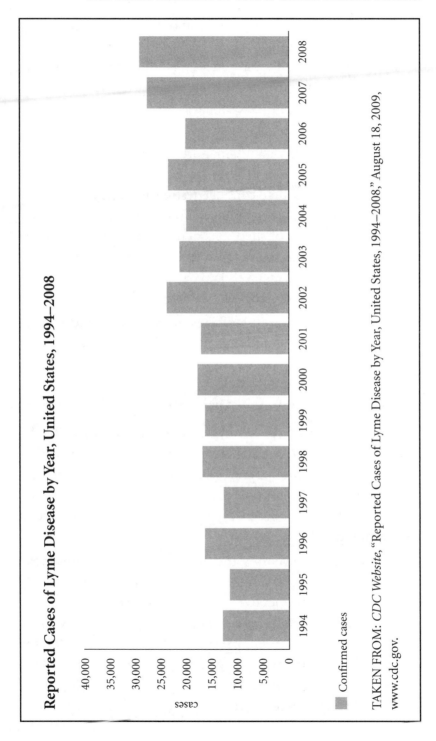

Reported Cases of Lyme Disease by Year, United States, 1994–2008

cases

Confirmed cases

TAKEN FROM: *CDC Website*, "Reported Cases of Lyme Disease by Year, United States, 1994–2008," August 18, 2009, www.cdc.gov.

Several years ago, a diagnostic laboratory marketed a one-step Lyme Urine Antigen Test [LUAT], data for which were presented at Lyme advocacy meetings and published in the journal of a Lyme advocacy group. The LUAT, however, was found to return a high rate of false-positive test results and has been discredited. . . .

In 2005, concerns about inappropriate laboratory testing prompted the CDC and FDA to issue a warning about "commercial laboratories that conduct testing for Lyme disease by using assays whose accuracy and clinical usefulness have not been adequately established. . . ." The CDC noted, "patients are encouraged to ask their physicians whether their testing . . . was performed using validated methods and whether results were interpreted using appropriate guidelines."

Some private practice physicians incorrectly diagnose Lyme disease in patients and subsequently treat them with inappropriate and ineffective regimens. . . .

## Overuse of Intravenous Antibiotics

Many Lyme disease activists insist Lyme disease is a difficult-to-treat, chronic infection that requires long-term consumption of powerful antibiotics. . . . Although decades of medical practice and recent clinical trials suggest otherwise, many Lyme patients still undergo expensive, long-term intravenous [IV] antibiotic treatments.

Outpatient intravenous therapy is a multi-billion-a-year business. It remains largely unregulated and can cost patients thousands of dollars per week. Price gouging, drug markups, kickbacks, and self-referral of patients by physicians with financial ties to infusion companies have occurred. In 1995, for example, Caremark, Inc., pled guilty to mail fraud charges for entering into illegal contracts with physicians by paying them to refer Medicaid patients to use Caremark's infusion products. In Michigan, prosecutors charged a physician and Caremark employees with scheming to over-bill Blue Cross/Blue Shield for drugs and equipment for patients with Lyme disease.

More recently [2007], *Forbes* magazine reported on the dangerous and expensive practices of so-called "Lyme Literate Doctors" (LLMD) who rely on powerful, long-term antibiotics to treat patients for presumptive Lyme disease.

The long-term intravenous antibiotic therapy administered to Lyme patients sometimes has disastrous results. During the early 1990s, the CDC described 25 cases of antibiotic-associated biliary [pertaining to the bile ducts] complications among persons with suspected disseminated Lyme disease. All patients had received intravenous ceftriaxone for an average of 28 days for suspected Lyme disease. (Ceftriaxone can form precipitates in the presence of bile salts. The resulting "sludge" can block the bile duct.) Twelve patients subsequently developed gallstones. Fourteen underwent cholecystectomy [removal of the gallbladder] to correct bile blockage. Twenty-two developed catheter-associated bloodstream infections. Yet most of the patients lacked documented evidence of disseminated Lyme disease or even antibodies to *B. burgdorferi*. In 2000, physicians reported the death of a 30-year-old woman who died from an infected intravenous setup that had been left in place for more than two years. She was being treated for a case of chronic Lyme disease. . . .

The risks and costs associated with such treatments were analyzed in a 1993 report whose authors concluded that for most patients with a positive Lyme antibody titer [test] and only symptoms of fatigue or nonspecific muscle pains, the risks and costs of intravenous antibiotic therapy exceed the benefits. Yet fourteen years later, these conclusions continue to be ignored by patients and physicians alike.

# Demands for Antibiotics

In an Internet newsgroup posting, a woman described being on intravenous antibiotic Rocephin for 4 weeks, developing gallstones, and switching to another antibiotic regimen for three more weeks. She also described a sudden high fever, anemia, low white cell count, systemic pain, heart rhythm disturbance, and neurologic symptoms. Such descriptions are common among devout Lyme patients and provide an unsettling view into the desperate and dangerous measures some people will take to treat suspected Lyme disease. The woman ended her account by writing that she had switched her medication to ciprofloxacin. This is a powerful antibiotic with side effects that may include acute psychosis and other neuropsychiatric reactions. Other online "antibiotic addicts" have confessed to using veterinary and aquarium antibiotics when they could not get physician prescriptions.

Another patient writing on the Internet said he was treated at a Mexican clinic where the doctor admitted that he and his staff knew little about Lyme disease. The patient wrote, "I started on IV Rocephin (two grams a day), and later added oral azithromycin. My symptoms did improve, but I soon hit a treatment plateau. We then tried IV doxycycline, but this made me sick to my stomach." He went on to describe a long list of other drugs (IV Claforan, Cefobid/Unisyn, Premaxin, a second round of Cefobid/Unisyn, and IV Zithromax), followed by bouts of "severe diarrhea" and phlebitis [swelling of veins]. Three months and some $25,000 later, DMSO [a drug used to deliver other medication through the skin] was added to another infusion of Zithromax.

Yet, the drug-seeking behaviors of self-described chronic Lyme patients and the prescribing practices of many "Lyme literate doctors" remain at odds with published research. Investigators carried out two treatment trials of patients claiming to suffer from chronic Lyme disease. They reported that "treatment with intravenous and oral antibiotics for 90 days did not improve symptoms more than placebo [a substance that has no medical effect]." Additional studies in Europe and the U.S. similarly found that: oral doxycycline is as effective as intravenous ceftriaxone in treating late-stage central nervous system infections; and additional antibiotics are not beneficial in improving cognitive function in patients with post-treatment chronic Lyme disease.

In October 2006, the Infectious Diseases Society of America [IDSA] published guidelines for effective intravenous (and oral) antibiotic regimens to treat various manifestations of Lyme disease. The European [Union] Concerted Action on Lyme Borreliosis (EUCALB) also has published recommendations for treating Lyme disease with various oral and intravenous antibiotics.

Published treatment guidelines provide important navigation aids for both physicians and patients. If you don't like the guidelines, however, there is nothing to stop you from making up your own. That's what one group of doctors did recently. They posted a set of Lyme disease diagnosis and treatment guidelines on a Web site, and then proceeded to follow the guidelines they had drafted. They referred to their guidelines as "evidence-based," but there is no evidence that the rationale for the guidelines has ever been validated in clinical trials or published in the professional literature, and there is no evidence that the guidelines have been endorsed by recognized medical societies such as the American Academy of Pediatrics or the American College of Physicians.

Indeed, the composers of these guidelines (copies of which they offered for $15) are a handful of private practice physicians and Lyme patient advocates. Some of these doctors have been disciplined by their state medical licensing boards. Many are not trained in infectious diseases and most have no research experience with Lyme disease. Still, that did not prevent them from having their guidelines listed in the National Guideline Clearinghouse or using that Web listing to suggest their guidelines are clinically appropriate and professionally endorsed. (The Clearinghouse listing is a directory, much like a phonebook, which neither endorses nor evaluates those listed. Unfortunately, this fact is not readily evident to patients looking for online information.)

## "Herxing"

Many patients who believe they have a chronic or persistent Lyme infection are willing to endure considerable discomfort in their effort to get rid of their symptoms. This behavior is fostered, in part, by the misguided belief that antibiotic therapies are not working unless they make the patient feel worse. These patients typically refer to this condition as "herxing," a colloquial term for the Jarisch-Herxheimer (J-H) reaction. This reaction is an acute response to the release of toxic or biologically active molecules from certain types of bacteria in the presence of some antibiotics.

About 10% of patients treated for early Lyme disease experience a J-H reaction involving chills, fever, muscle pains, rapid heartbeat, and slight lowering of blood pressure during the first 24 hours of antibiotic therapy. These symptoms usually last for several hours, and require little more than aspirin and bed rest. Yet many Lyme newsgroup participants write about a "herx" beginning days or weeks after the start of antibiotic therapy, and "herxing" for weeks at a time—often in a cyclic fashion. "Herxing" events have even been likened to an "exorcism" that is "a necessary evil to be endured." Some of these patients are likely to be suffering from the side effects of their inappropriately prescribed antibiotics. It is also safe to assume that the mistaken belief that Lyme treatment involves temporary worsening will lead some people to neglect other illnesses. Neurological symptoms, blurred vision, gastrointestinal upset, vomiting, and palpitations, for example, should be reported to a physician, not posted on the Internet with a request for comments. . . .

## Political Aspects

The fact that Lyme disease is readily curable has not discouraged the formation of over a hundred support groups and nonprofit foundations, some with ties to intravenous services, Lyme diagnostic labs, and physicians specializing in private Lyme disease practices. These groups and their ardent followers have used the Internet and other media to barrage politicians and the general public with misinformation, dire personal stories, rumors, and exaggerated claims about thousands of people being maimed, killed and bankrupted each year by Lyme disease. The core message is that Lyme is a deadly chronic disease that requires long-term antibiotic therapy paid for by insurance companies.

Despite the alleged frequency of chronic Lyme disease, clinical trials funded by the National Institutes of Health (NIH) were hampered by a lack of patients who met evidence-based medical criteria for Lyme disease. A third trial at Columbia University had to modify its patient entry criteria in order to find enough patients to carry out the study. The reality is Lyme remains a common bacterial infection that is antibiotic-responsive, nonfatal, non-communicable, and geographically and seasonally limited in range.

Still, support groups and individual patients have created numerous Web sites that contain unsubstantiated claims, inaccurate medical information, and personal testimonies for the dubious treatments described above. Indeed, the Internet has provided a powerful mechanism for organizing patients and presenting poorly documented information to the public and the press. And as the owner of one Lyme diagnostic lab recently said, "Patients, because of the Internet, have become my best salesmen."

Internet newsgroups also have posted violent polemics against physicians and researchers who disagree with their claims and concerns. Research reports that run counter to the claims of Lyme activists are denounced and their authors accused of incompetence and financial conflicts of interest. Magazines and news organizations whose stories on Lyme disease are not sufficiently hysterical are barraged with e-mail complaints and urged to contact certain organizations for "the truth." Protests have been organized to denounce Yale University because, according to the protesters, Yale "ridicules people with Lyme disease, presents misleading information, minimizes the severity of the illness, endorses inadequate, outdated treatment protocols, excludes opposing viewpoints, and ignores conflicts of interest."

Researchers have been harassed, threatened, and stalked. A petition circulated on the Web called for changes in the way the disease is routinely treated and the way insurance companies cover those treatments. Less radical groups have had their meetings invaded and disrupted by militant Lyme protesters. In October 2006, the New Jersey–based Lyme Disease Association (LDA) led a series of protests at New York Medical College to denounce the updated Lyme disease treatment guidelines published by the IDSA. The LDA organized another online petition against the guidelines, and a related LLMD organization demanded the treatment guidelines be retracted. Evidently, they were worried the guidelines would be accepted by insurance companies and therefore cut into their private practice profits.

In November 2006, Lyme activists persuaded the Connecticut attorney general, Richard Blumenthal, to file a Civil Investigative Demand (CID) to look into possible antitrust violations by the IDSA during the drafting of the treatment guidelines. A few weeks later, the activists persuaded congressional representative Chris Smith (R-NJ) to write a letter to the CDC director questioning the CDC's support of the IDSA guidelines and suggesting CDC needed to show support for alternative guidelines developed by activists and the private practice, for-profit physicians who treat them.

The CDC declined to do so. Moreover, few lawyers and physicians believe Blumenthal's quixotic use of antitrust law to intimidate a nonprofit professional society into changing or withdrawing voluntary clinical guidelines is going to affect the treatment of Lyme disease. Yet, these events demonstrate the power of Internet-connected activists to mobilize political power in order to question evidence-based medicine and peer-reviewed scientific research.

> "So here's what I did—and what you should do too. I asked my doctor for an emergency supply of antibiotics that would get me through the first week or so of a crisis."

# Individuals Should Stockpile Antibiotics in Case of Anthrax Attack

*Stewart Baker*

*Stewart Baker was the first assistant secretary for policy at the U.S. Department of Homeland Security. In the following viewpoint, he notes that the Barack Obama administration is relying on the postal service to deliver emergency antibiotics in case of a biological anthrax attack. Baker argues that this method is inadequate. Instead, he says, individuals should ask their doctors for emergency antibiotics to be used in case of a biological attack. Baker says that, despite official disapproval, individual stockpiling will be more efficient and safer than relying on other distribution methods.*

Stewart Baker, "I'm Sorry Sir. There's Still Postage Due on Yours," skatingonstlits.com, January 3, 2010. Reproduced by permission.

As you read, consider the following questions:

1. If we suffer an anthrax attack, how quickly does Baker say everyone exposed will need antibiotics?
2. According to Baker, what delivery method would work really well in the event of an emergency?
3. Why does Baker say that stockpiling antibiotics is socially responsible?

When was the last time you gave the US Postal Service responsibility for delivering a package that absolutely had to get to the recipient as fast as possible?

Right. I don't remember either.

## Using the Mail to Deliver Antibiotics

The [Barack Obama] administration, though, has nothing but faith in the Postal Service. In fact, it's willing to make a big bet on the Postal Service's nimbleness, sense of urgency, and dedication to duty.

And when I say big, I mean really big; it's willing to bet your life on it.

Literally. If we suffer an anthrax [a disease caused by a deadly bacteria, which can be used as a biological weapon] attack, everyone who's been exposed will need antibiotics within three days of the attack. That's within two days of our discovery of the attack, if we're lucky. Every day of delay after that is a death sentence for roughly five or ten percent of those exposed.

How will we get antibiotics in the hands of what could be hundreds of thousands of really worried people? The administration's answer is contained in an executive order released quietly last week: We'll get the Postal Service to do it. Of course they're already demanding armed protection, so we'll send local law enforcement officers with them.

Stop for a moment to imagine the scene. Postal workers will be asked to drive into contaminated neighborhoods even though they can't be sure their countermeasures will work against whatever strain has been spread there. The neighborhoods are full of people desperate to get antibiotics, so for protection, the postal workers will first have to meet up with guys with guns whom they've never seen before. They'll collect antibiotics from pickup points that they may or may not have gone to before. They'll meet the guys with guns there, or someplace else that may have to be made up at the last minute. Then they'll start out on routes that almost certainly will be new to them. As they go, they will seamlessly and fairly make decisions about whether to deliver the antibiotics to homes where no one is present, to rural mailboxes that may or may not be easily rifled, to people on the street who claim to live down the way, to the guys with guns who are riding with them and have friends or family at risk, and to men in big cars who offer cash for anything that falls off the truck.

And all this will put antibiotics in the hands of every single exposed person within 48 hours, from a no-notice standing start.

Yeah, that should work.

I don't mean to be flip. . . . The fact is that no delivery method will work really well, and so, as a fallback, the Postal Service may be our best option.

That said, no one but an idiot would bet their children's lives on that option.

## Ask Your Doctor for Emergency Antibiotics

So here's what I did—and what you should do too. I asked my doctor for an emergency supply of antibiotics that would get me through the first week or so of a crisis. I promised not to take the antibiotics irresponsibly for colds or other viral infections. And I was ready to change doctors over the issue.

I got the prescription.

Some public health officials may try to make you feel guilty about "hoarding" antibiotics or contributing to antibi-

## The Danger of Bioterrorism

We [the Commission on the Prevention of Weapons of Mass Destruction Proliferation and Terrorism] stated that terrorists are more likely to obtain and use a biological weapon than a nuclear weapon. In the late fall of 2008, we concluded that unless we act urgently and decisively, it was more likely than not that terrorists would use a weapon of mass destruction somewhere in the world by the end [of] 2013. On December 2, 2008, the Director of National Intelligence publicly agreed with this assessment.

*Bob Graham and Jim Talent,*
*"Bioterrorism: Redefining Prevention,"*
*Commission on the Prevention of Weapons of*
*Mass Destruction Proliferation and Terrorism,*
*June 2009. www.preventwmd.gov.*

otic resistance. Poppycock. If you buy while supplies are plentiful, you're actually making a bigger market for these products and contributing to the maintenance of production capability. And if you don't take them irresponsibly, you won't affect resistance.

In fact, you're even being socially responsible. If we do suffer an anthrax attack and the Postal Service is having trouble keeping up, a sure bet if ever there was one, you can defer your delivery in favor of someone who has no stash. You'll take a bit of strain off a system that is going to need all the relief it can get.

(In addition to the glow of virtue, you can feel a bit of that leftover '60s civil disobedience thrill. When I tried to put this home stockpile advice in a speech toward the tail end of the last administration [the George W. Bush administration], I was informed by the lawyers that advocating an unapproved use of prescription medicine is a criminal offense under FDA [U.S. Food and Drug Administration] law. And, while taking antibiotics for an anthrax attack is an approved use, getting antibiotics *in case of* an anthrax attack is not an approved use. I think that may mean that this post is, um, a felony. If so, well, power to the people and come and get me, coppers!)

What's unfortunate about the executive order is that there's not a hint that the administration is considering the home stockpile as the first and best way to prepare for a possible attack. If that's really the government's last word on the subject, it's like telling passengers that the best response to an air hijacking is to sit tight and wait for the authorities to arrive.

It's insufferably paternalistic and it's bad advice.

The only good part about it is, no one is going to listen.

> *"One concern was that people wouldn't understand how to properly store or use the drugs, potentially leading to greater antibiotic resistance, possibly dangerous side effects, and a false sense of security."*

# Individuals Should Not Stockpile Antibiotics in Case of Anthrax Attack

*David Malakoff*

*David Malakoff is a science writer whose work has appeared in various outlets including* Science *and National Public Radio. In the following viewpoint, he reports that public health experts are concerned about government promotion of home stockpiling of antibiotics. The experts worry that people may misuse antibiotics, resulting in increased antibiotic resistance, side effects, or a false sense of security. The scientists recommend that the government take care to consult with health professionals before encouraging individuals to stockpile antibiotics.*

As you read, consider the following questions:

1. What is the National Biodefense Science Board?

David Malakoff, "Stockpiling Antibioterror Drugs May Be Unsafe, Experts Warn," *Science*NOW, August 13, 2008. Copyright © 2008 by AAAS. Reproduced by permission.

2. What preparations have federal officials been making to defend the public since the 2001 anthrax attacks, according to Malakoff?

3. Why would it take several years to prepare government MedKits, according to Brooke Courtney?

Public health experts are warning senior U.S. officials against moving ahead with a plan to give the public advice on how to stockpile antibiotics against a bioterror attack. The move would be "unwise" because it could promote unsafe uses of the drugs, says the National Biodefense Science Board (NBSB), a panel of independent experts that advises the government.

## The Government Should Not Encourage Stockpiling

The warning, included in a letter soon to be sent to Michael Leavitt, the secretary of the Department of Health & Human Services (HHS), was prompted by the circulation late last month [July 2008] of a draft HHS fact sheet. It answers 16 questions about stockpiling drugs that could be used after an attack with the deadly bacteria that cause anthrax [a dangerous disease]. Although the document warns that "home storage of antibiotics involves risks that you should consider very seriously," members of the science board fear it would be seen as government endorsement of stockpiling—which some critics say may not work and could create other problems.

"The board isn't saying this should never be done, but we are saying you need to sit down and understand all the ramifications before you go any further," NBSB head M. Patricia Quinlisk told *Science*NOW. Quinlisk, a physician, is medical director of Iowa's public health department. HHS officials were not available for comment as *Science*NOW went to press.

Since the 2001 anthrax attacks[1], federal officials have been making preparations to defend the public against a similar bacterial onslaught. They've stockpiled huge caches of antibiotics near major cities, for instance, so that they can be distributed quickly during a crisis. They have also begun to develop prepackaged emergency packets of drugs—called "MedKits"—that families could buy and store. And some officials have argued that people should go to a doctor, get a prescription for antibiotics, and then tuck them away at home.

That strategy "could reduce your need to depend upon public health agencies as they try to get antibiotics to everyone at risk during an anthrax emergency," the fact sheet, dated 31 July [2008], states. It also specifies which drugs work against anthrax and warns that giving them to children can be dangerous.

## People May Misuse Antibiotics

But the board believes the government is moving too fast. At a meeting on 18 June, several board members—and officials from the Centers for Disease Control and Prevention and the U.S. Food and Drug Administration—raised serious concerns about stockpiling after HHS officials described their work on the issue. According to meeting minutes, one concern was that people wouldn't understand how to properly store or use the drugs, potentially leading to greater antibiotic resistance, possibly dangerous side effects, and a false sense of security. Another was that doctors and public health officials hadn't been fully consulted.

Quinlisk says that some of those concerns were reflected in the draft fact sheet that HHS staff produced last month but that it still isn't ready for public release. "We urge you not to move precipitously to promote home stockpiling before the scientific questions can be answered," their current letter

---

1. In 2001, letters containing anthrax spores were mailed to media offices and to senators, killing five people.

concludes. "There is a high risk of providing a confusing message that does not have the endorsement of experts in public health, biodefense, and infectious disease, nor of the majority of medical practitioners."

Other experts agree. "The board does raise some very good points," says Brooke Courtney, who analyzes biodefense policy for the Center for Biosecurity at the University of Pittsburgh Medical Center in Pennsylvania. The draft fact sheet, she says, "could be very confusing for the general public." And she says the dangers of trying to properly use antibiotics "when you are scared and under a lot [of] stress" shouldn't be underestimated, especially given the often confusing directions on pill bottles.

Still, Courtney says that the government needs to be looking at creative ways of preparing the public for a bioterror attack. For instance, she says the carefully packaged MedKits that the government is developing "could be a really useful approach." But she notes that it could be several years before the kits are available, because they need to undergo careful testing and government approval.

# Periodical Bibliography

*The following articles have been selected to supplement the diverse views presented in this chapter.*

| American Lyme Disease Foundation | "Frequently Asked Questions," January 5, 2010. www.aldf.com. |
|---|---|
| Arthritis Foundation | "Using Antibiotics to Treat Arthritis," *Arthritis Today*, n.d. www.arthritis.org. |
| Allison Aubrey | "Doubts Raised over Antibiotic Use for Acne," *NPR Online*, January 19, 2006. www.npr.org. |
| William J. Bicknell | "How Best to Fight Against Bioterrorism," Cato Institute, August 5, 2003. www.cato.org. |
| Melissa Dahl | "Super Acne? Drug-Resistant Zits on the Rise," MSNBC.com, April 13, 2009. www.msnbc.msn .com. |
| Homeland Security News Wire | "Letter Carriers May Deliver Antibiotics During Bioterror Attack," October 2, 2008. http:// homelandsecuritynewswire.com. |
| *Infection Control Today* | "Review Panel Upholds Lyme Disease Treatment Guidelines," April 22, 2010. www.infec tioncontroltoday.com. |
| Stuart B. Levy | "Risks of Stockpiling Antibiotics to Counter Bioterrorism," Alliance for the Prudent Use of Antibiotics (APUA), October 15, 2001. www .tufts.edu/med/apua/home.html. |
| The Road Back Foundation | "Rheumatoid Arthritis," n.d. www.road back.org. |
| Tevi Troy | "Preparing for Bioterrorism," *Weekly Standard*, February 23, 2010. www.weeklystandard.com. |
| WebMD Arthritis Health Center | "Antibiotics for Lyme Disease," September 3, 2008. http://arthritis.webmd.com. |

# CHAPTER 4

# What Are Some of the Dangers of Using Antibiotics?

# Chapter Preface

One of the dangers of using antibiotics is that over time bacteria will develop resistance to those antibiotics. When this happens with tuberculosis bacteria, the result is extensively drug-resistant tuberculosis, or XDR-TB, a very dangerous disease.

Tuberculosis, or TB, is a bacterial infectious disease, which usually strikes the lungs but can also infect other organs of the body. It is spread by "breathing infected air through close contact" according to George Schiffman in an article on Medi cineNet.com. Schiffman notes that tuberculosis is a serious health problem in many parts of the world, including the former Soviet Union, Southeast Asia, Africa, and prison populations worldwide. The spread of HIV [human immunodeficiency virus] through the 2000s greatly increased the prevalence of TB, as those with immune systems weakened by AIDS [acquired immunodeficiency syndrome] are especially susceptible to tuberculosis.

An October 2006 fact sheet by the World Health Organization (WHO) Stop TB Department explains that "TB can usually be treated with a course of four standard, or first-line, anti-TB drugs." When these antibiotics are misused, however, TB can develop resistance, requiring the use of second-line antibiotics. When those drugs are misused, multidrug resistant TB (MDR-TB) can develop. A March 2010 WHO fact sheet further explains, "Drug-resistant TB is caused by inconsistent or partial treatment, when patients do not take all their medicines regularly for the required period because they start to feel better, because doctors and health workers prescribe the wrong treatment regimens, or because the drug supply is unreliable." Whatever causes it, however, MDR-TB is extremely dangerous, with a cure possible for only "up to 30% of affected people," according to WHO.

XDR-TB is not common, but where it does occur, it presents major challenges to doctors and public health officials. For instance, in South Africa, authorities have imprisoned those suffering from XDR-TB against their will to stop the almost incurable disease from spreading. In a March 25, 2008, article in the *New York Times*, Celia W. Dugger reported, "The Jose Pearson TB Hospital [in Port Elizabeth, South Africa] is like a prison for the sick. It is encircled by three fences topped with coils of razor wire to keep patients infected with lethal strains of tuberculosis from escaping." Jerome Amir Singh, Ross Upshur, and Nesri Padayatchi writing in a January 2007 article in *PLoS Medicine* said that in South Africa "XDR-TB is a serious global health threat. It has the potential to derail the global efforts to contain HIV/AIDS, as broadly disseminated XDR-TB will prove to be a much more serious public health threat owing to its mode of transmission." They called for new diagnostic tests and major quarantine efforts, concluding, "Ultimately in such crises, the interests of public health must prevail over the rights of the individual." The viewpoints in this chapter examine some of the dangers of using or misusing antibiotics in relation to treating infectious diseases.

| "This study provides more reason for people to use antibiotics wisely."

# Antibiotics May Be Linked to Breast Cancer

*National Cancer Institute*

*The National Cancer Institute (NCI) is a U.S. government project focusing on cancer research. In the following viewpoint, the NCI discusses a study that found a link between antibiotic use and an increased risk of breast cancer in women. The NCI notes that the study does not show a cause-and-effect relationship between antibiotics and cancer and says that women should still take antibiotics for bacterial infections when the drugs are prescribed by doctors. However, NCI argues that the study is another reason why people should take antibiotics only as directed.*

As you read, consider the following questions:

1. According to the study, women who took what amount of antibiotics were at how much more risk of getting breast cancer than women who took no antibiotics?

2. What does the NCI say women who take antibiotics long term for acne or bladder infections should do?

National Cancer Institute, "Study Shows Link Between Antibiotic Use and Increased Risk of Breast Cancer," December 29, 2004.

3. What factors other than antibiotic use does the NCI say may have caused the increased risk of breast cancer?

- The authors of the study [published in the *Journal of the American Medical Association (JAMA)* in February 2004] found that antibiotic use was associated with an increased risk of breast cancer. The more antibiotics the women in the study had used, the higher their risk of breast cancer.

- These results do not mean that antibiotics *cause* cancer, only that there is an association between the two.

- Breast cancer is the second leading cause of cancer deaths among women in the United States. An estimated 40,110 women will die of the disease this year.

- Antibiotics are used extensively in this country and in many parts of the world. They can have substantial benefits when used to treat bacterial infections. Antibiotics also are overused in many parts of the world, contributing to the growth of antibiotic resistance. This study provides more reason to use antibiotics wisely.

- More studies must be done to understand what causes the increased risk of breast cancer with antibiotic use.

## A Link Between Breast Cancer and Antibiotics

*What were the basic findings of this study?*

Antibiotic use is associated with an increased risk of breast cancer. The authors found that the more antibiotics the women in the study had used, the higher their risk of breast cancer.

*What do these results mean?*

These study results do not mean that antibiotics *cause* cancer. These results only show that there is an association between the two. More research is necessary to learn if there is a direct cause-and-effect relationship.

*What specifically did the authors find?*

The authors found that women who took antibiotics for more than 500 days—or had more than 25 prescriptions—over an average period of 17 years had twice the risk of breast cancer as women who had taken no antibiotics. The risk was smaller for women who took fewer antibiotics, but even women who had between one and 25 prescriptions over an average period of 17 years had an increased risk; they were about 1.5 times more likely to be diagnosed with breast cancer than those women who didn't take any antibiotics. The authors found the increase in risk across all classes of antibiotics that they studied.

*Should women not take antibiotics, even if their doctor tells them that they have a bacterial infection?*

No. There is no reason to avoid antibiotics for bacterial infections; antibiotics can have a significant health benefit for such infections. However, this study provides more reason for people to use antibiotics wisely—to take antibiotics only for bacterial infections and not to use them to try to treat common colds and other illnesses caused by viruses.

*What should women do who take antibiotics long term for conditions such as acne or recurrent bladder infections?*

Women should talk to their health care providers about the risks and benefits of antibiotic use for their condition(s). Antibiotics should be used as recommended only when patients and their physicians have determined that they are the best treatment. In addition, women should follow their doctor's recommendations regarding breast cancer screening.

## Is There a Cause-and-Effect Relationship?

*Is it possible that other risk factors for breast cancer could explain the increased risk seen in this study?*

Factors such as age, reproductive and menstrual history, lifestyle factors, use of hormone therapy, and high breast density, among other factors, can affect breast cancer risk. The authors designed the *JAMA* study in such a way as to minimize the chance that these and other factors would affect the results. They matched the "cases"—women who were diagnosed with breast cancer—and "controls"—women who did not have breast cancer—with regard to these factors. For example, 23.7 percent of cases had a body mass index of more than 30.0 kg/m² and almost the same number (21.8 percent) of controls had the same body mass index, lowering the chance that the higher risk of breast cancer seen in the case group was due to obesity. . . .

*What factors, other than antibiotic use, might explain why the women in this study have an increased risk of breast cancer?*

It is possible that the conditions that required the women to take the antibiotics might have increased their risk of breast cancer. For example, a weakened immune system might lead both to infections that require antibiotics and to cancer development.

It is also possible that women who have not taken any antibiotics may be a uniquely healthy group in terms of general well-being or lifestyle factors, possibly accounting for some of the increased breast cancer risk that the authors observed among antibiotic users.

*Alternatively, if there is a cause-and-effect relationship, how do researchers think that antibiotic use might lead to breast cancer?*

Based on current understanding, there are a couple of possible explanations for why antibiotics might lead to breast cancer. One theory is that antibiotics can affect bacteria in the intestine, which may impact the way certain foods that protect against cancer are broken down in the body. Another possibility is that antibiotics can affect the body's immune response and response to inflammation, both of which could be related

## More Antibiotics, More Cancer

In this population-based case-control study, we found that increasing cumulative days of antibiotic use and increasing cumulative number of antibiotic prescriptions were associated with increased risk of incident breast cancer, after controlling for age and length of enrollment [in the health care plan studied]. Increasing cumulative days of antibiotic use was also associated with death due to breast cancer, controlling for age, length of enrollment, and even use of postmenopausal hormones. All classes of antibiotics were associated with increased risk.

*Christine M. Velicer et al.,*
*"Antibiotic Use in Relation to the Risk of Breast Cancer,"*
JAMA, *February 18, 2004, vol. 291, no. 7., p. 833.*

to the development of cancer. Many more studies are necessary to better understand how or why antibiotics could lead to cancer.

## About the Study

*Why did the authors conduct this study?*

Breast cancer is the second leading cause of cancer deaths among women in the United States. It is estimated that 40,110 women will die of the disease in 2004. In addition, breast cancer is the most common cancer in women worldwide.

Antibiotics are used—and overused—extensively throughout the world to treat many conditions, illnesses, and diseases. For example, more than 70 percent of women in the study had used between one and 25 prescriptions for antibiotics in the past 17 years. Only 18 percent of women in the study had not filled any antibiotic prescriptions during their enrollment in the health plan. About 2 percent to 3 percent of the women in the study had used more than 50 prescriptions over an average time period of 17 years. . . .

The idea that antibiotics might increase cancer risk was first proposed decades ago. Before this study in the *Journal of the American Medical Association,* there had been only one study to examine the association between antibiotics and cancer risk, and it also focused on breast cancer. That study, of almost 10,000 women in Finland, was less thorough in its evaluation of antibiotic use, but still found that increased antibiotic use was associated with an increased risk of breast cancer.

*How was this* JAMA *study conducted?*

The authors used computerized pharmacy and breast cancer screening databases at Group Health Cooperative in Seattle, a large, nonprofit health plan in Washington State. They compared the antibiotic use of 2,266 women with breast cancer to similar information from 7,953 women without breast cancer. All the women in the study were age 20 and older, and the researchers examined a wide variety of the most frequently prescribed antibiotic medications.

*Who funded this study?*

The study was funded by the National Cancer Institute and by the Gustavus and Louise Pfeiffer Research Foundation.

## About Antibiotics

*What conditions are antibiotics used to treat?*

Antibiotics are used to fight bacterial infections. They are commonly prescribed to treat bladder and respiratory infections, acne, and rosacea, among other conditions. Rosacea is a disease that affects the skin and sometimes the eyes, causing redness, pimples and, in advanced stages, thickened skin.

*What should people know about antibiotics?*

Antibiotics can show substantial results when used to treat bacterial infections and should be taken exactly as prescribed by a health care provider. It is important to note, however, that antibiotics won't help at all against the flu or the common cold, which are caused by viruses, not bacteria. Over the past decade, overuse of antibiotics has become a serious problem. According to the Centers for Disease Control and Prevention (CDC), tens of millions of antibiotics are prescribed for viral infections that are not treatable with antibiotics, contributing to the alarming growth of antibiotic resistance. . . .

*What studies must be done to understand more about the link between antibiotic use and breast cancer?*

Scientists must conduct additional studies to determine what causes the increased risk of breast cancer with antibiotic use. In addition, more studies are necessary to determine whether the risk of breast cancer is higher for women who used antibiotics at a certain period of their life, such as during adolescence or during pregnancy, or whether women who used antibiotics for specific conditions have a higher risk than women who used the drugs to treat other conditions.

> "No evidence was presented that antibiotics were the biological cause of any of the cases of breast cancer considered in the study."

# Antibiotics Do Not Contribute to Breast Cancer

*Steven Milloy*

*Steven Milloy is an adjunct author at the Cato Institute and author of* Junk Science Judo: Self-Defense Against Health Scares and Scams. *In the following viewpoint, he argues that a study linking breast cancer to antibiotics does not in fact show that antibiotics cause breast cancer. Further, he argues that the study's data is too weak to show any convincing link at all between breast cancer and antibiotics. Milloy concludes that there is no need for further research on this topic and suggests that the researchers involved are trying to stir up controversy to obtain more grant funding.*

As you read, consider the following questions:

1. Why does Milloy say that it is not surprising that no evidence was presented to show that antibiotics were the cause of breast cancer?

2. What was the average age of the study subjects, how long had they been enrolled in the studied health plan, and why does Milloy argue that this is a problem for the study data?

3. Why does Milloy argue that the researchers do not really know how many antibiotics the studied subjects took?

Antibiotic use increases breast cancer risk, according to a new study. But after scrutinizing the study, I'm leaning toward linking grant-hungry researchers and a publicity-hungry medical journal with reprehensible sensationalism.

## No Evidence That Antibiotics Cause Breast Cancer

The study in the Feb. 18 [2004] issue of the *Journal of the American Medical Association* reported all levels of antibiotic use were associated with increased risk of breast cancer and death from breast cancer.

The study triggered an avalanche of "Antibiotics Linked to Breast Cancer" news reports, most of which were sensibly tempered with "don't panic," "don't stop taking antibiotics" and "more research is needed" caveats.

Researchers compared antibiotic use among 2,266 women with breast cancer and 7,953 women without breast cancer, all of whom belonged to a large health plan in western Washington State. Data on antibiotic use was obtained from the health plan's records.

Antibiotic use for 1 to 50 cumulative days reportedly was associated with a 50 percent increase in breast cancer risk. Antibiotic use for more than 1,000 cumulative days reportedly was associated with a 100 percent increase in risk. The results sound scary, but here's why they're not.

No evidence was presented that antibiotics were the biological cause of any of the cases of breast cancer considered in the study. This is no surprise since no demonstrable biological explanation exists as to why antibiotics would cause cancer in the first place.

Without a plausible biological link between antibiotic use and breast cancer, the researchers relied exclusively on statistical analysis, a potentially useful tool if the data analyzed are of reasonable quality. These study data, however, fall way short.

The average study subject was about 60 years old. But study subjects who had taken antibiotics had been enrolled in the health plan for only about 20 years on average. Since the sole source for data on antibiotic use was the health plan's records, about 40 years of data, on average, about potential antibiotic use were missing for each study subject.

Even more data are missing for the 18 percent of the study subjects who supposedly never took antibiotics. These women had been in the health plan for only about 10 years on average.

## The Data Is Inadequate

But the mere fact they didn't take antibiotics while enrolled in the health plan doesn't mean they didn't take antibiotics before enrollment. Indeed, some of the supposed "never users" could actually have been extremely heavy users of antibiotics prior to enrollment in the health plan.

Since the vast majority of Americans have taken antibiotics at some point, it's difficult to believe so many of the study subjects had never taken antibiotics.

This is a crucial data gap, since the researchers claim even a single day of antibiotic use increased breast cancer risk. The absence of complete data on lifetime antibiotic use renders comparisons between users and "nonusers" meaningless.

The study data are also faulty in terms of level of exposure to antibiotics. The researchers assumed exposure to antibiotics could be measured either by number of antibiotic prescriptions written or by the number of days prescribed for antibiotic use according to prescription records.

But patients commonly fail to complete courses of antibiotics prescribed by their doctors. Patients with a prescription for 10 days of antibiotics may feel better after just a few days and cease taking their medicine. A 10-day prescription, therefore, doesn't necessarily mean 10 days of use. It may, in fact, mean much less use.

So the researchers really can't say more antibiotic use increases breast cancer risk because they really don't know who took more antibiotics.

Though the researchers acknowledged their study doesn't prove antibiotics cause breast cancer and that many other possible explanations for their reported results could exist, they called for more research—that is, more taxpayer-funded research like this study.

That's pretty twisted, though. The researchers used obviously deficient data to stir up a frightening, but dubious, controversy they hope to milk for continued research funding.

Antibiotics have been used since the 1940s—to the great benefit of public health. More than 100 million prescriptions are written in the U.S. every year. If antibiotics were a cancer risk, it's very likely such a link would have been observed long ago.

Finally, the *Journal of the American Medical Association* should be ashamed for scaring the public about antibiotics with such a flimsy study. Five years ago, *Journal* editor George Lundberg was fired for trying to garner headlines with another sensational but absurd study. Heads should roll again.

> *"Norwegian doctors prescribe fewer antibiotics than any other country, so people do not have a chance to develop resistance to them."*

# MRSA Proliferates Because of the Overuse of Antibiotics

*Martha Mendoza and Margie Mason*

*Martha Mendoza is an award-winning writer for the Associated Press (AP); Margie Mason is a health and science writer. In the following viewpoint, the authors report on Norway's efforts to get rid of methicillin-resistant* Staphylococcus aureus *(MRSA), an antibiotic-resistant bacterial infection that has killed thousands in the United States. They note that Norway has cut back drastically on the use of antibiotics and has instituted stricter regulations on hygiene in hospitals. As a result, the authors say, MRSA rates have plummeted. The authors conclude that other nations should follow Norway's example in order to reduce MRSA outbreaks.*

As you read, consider the following questions:

1. According to the authors, how does Norway regulate drug advertisements to reduce MRSA?

2. Which country is the world leader in MRSA, and what percentage of staph infections in that country are attributable to MRSA, according to the authors?

3. What controls does Dr. Barry Farr believe the CDC must introduce to control MRSA?

A ker University Hospital is a dingy place to heal. The floors are streaked and scratched. A light layer of dust coats the blood pressure monitors. A faint stench of urine and bleach wafts from a pile of soiled bedsheets dropped in a corner.

Look closer, however, at a microscopic level, and this place is pristine. There is no sign of a dangerous and contagious staph [a kind of bacteria] infection that killed tens of thousands of patients in the most sophisticated hospitals of Europe, North America and Asia this year [2009], soaring virtually unchecked.

The reason: Norwegians stopped taking so many drugs.

Twenty-five years ago, Norwegians were also losing their lives to this bacteria. But Norway's public health system fought back with an aggressive program that made it the most infection-free country in the world. A key part of that program was cutting back severely on the use of antibiotics.

Now a spate of new studies from around the world proves that Norway's model can be replicated with extraordinary success, and public health experts are saying these deaths—19,000 in the U.S each year alone, more than from AIDS—are unnecessary.

"It's a very sad situation that in some places so many are dying from this, because we have shown here in Norway that methicillin-resistant *Staphylococcus aureus* (MRSA) can be controlled, and with not too much effort," said Jan Hendrik-Binder, Oslo's MRSA medical adviser. "But you have to take it seriously, you have to give it attention, and you must not give up."

The World Health Organization says antibiotic resistance is one of the leading public health threats on the planet.

Now, in Norway's simple solution, there's a glimmer of hope.

## "Golden Rules"

Dr. John Birger Haug shuffles down Aker's scuffed corridors, patting the pocket of his baggy white scrubs. "My bible," the infectious disease specialist says, pulling out a little red antibiotic guide that details this country's impressive MRSA solution.

It's what's missing from this book—an array of antibiotics—that makes it so remarkable.

"There are times I must show these golden rules to our doctors and tell them they cannot prescribe something, but our patients do not suffer more and our nation, as a result, is mostly infection free," he says.

Norway's model is surprisingly straightforward.

- Norwegian doctors prescribe fewer antibiotics than any other country, so people do not have a chance to develop resistance to them.

- Patients with MRSA are isolated and medical staff who test positive stay at home.

- Doctors track each case of MRSA by its individual strain, interviewing patients about where they've been and who they've been with, testing anyone who has been in contact with them.

Haug unlocks the dispensary, a small room lined with boxes of pills, bottles of syrups and tubes of ointment. What's here? Medicines considered obsolete in many developed countries. What's not? Some of the newest, most expensive antibiotics, which aren't even registered for use in Norway, "because if we have them here, doctors will use them," he says.

Norwegians are sanguine about their coughs and colds, toughing it out through low-grade infections.

## Estimated MRSA Infections and Estimated Deaths in the U.S. by Age, 2005

|  | Estimated MRSA Infections | Estimated Deaths |
|---|---|---|
| Under 1 | 950 | 80 |
| 1 | 160 | 0 |
| 2–4 | 290 | 10 |
| 5–17 | 730 | 60 |
| 18–34 | 7,050 | 460 |
| 35–49 | 16,100 | 1,400 |
| 50–64 | 22,120 | 3,640 |
| 65 and over | 46,970 | 13,000 |

TAKEN FROM: R. Monina Klevens, et. al. "Invasive Methicillin-Resistant *Staphylococcus aureus* Infections in the United States," *JAMA*, October 17, 2007, Vol 298, No. 15, p. 1767.

"We don't throw antibiotics at every person with a fever. We tell them to hang on, wait and see, and we give them a Tylenol to feel better," Haug says.

Convenience stores in downtown Oslo are stocked with an amazing and colorful array—42 different brands at one downtown 7-Eleven—of soothing, but non-medicated, lozenges, sprays and tablets. All workers are paid on days they, or their children, stay home sick. And drug makers aren't allowed to advertise, reducing patient demands for prescription drugs.

In fact, most marketing here sends the opposite message: "Penicillin is not a cough medicine," says the tissue packet on the desk of Norway's MRSA control director, Dr. Petter Elstrom.

He recognizes his country is "unique in the world and best in the world" when it comes to MRSA. Fewer than 1 percent of health care providers are positive carriers of MRSA staph.

But Elstrom worries about the bacteria slipping in through other countries. Last year almost every diagnosed case in Norway came from someone who had been abroad.

"So far we've managed to contain it, but if we lose this, it will be a huge problem," he said.

Forty years ago, a new spectrum of antibiotics enchanted public health officials, quickly quelling one infection after another. In wealthier countries that could afford them, patients and providers came to depend on antibiotics. Trouble was, the more antibiotics are consumed, the more resistant bacteria develop.

Norway responded swiftly to initial MRSA outbreaks in the 1980s by cutting antibiotic use. Thus while they got ahead of the infection, the rest of the world fell behind.

In Norway, MRSA has accounted for less than 1 percent of staph infections for years. That compares to 80 percent in Japan, the world leader in MRSA; 44 percent in Israel; and 38 percent in Greece.

In the U.S, cases have soared and MRSA cost $6 billion last year. Rates have gone up from 2 percent in 1974 to 63 percent in 2004. And in the United Kingdom, they rose from about 2 percent in the early 1990s to about 45 percent.

About 1 percent of people in developed countries carry MRSA on their skin. Usually harmless, the bacteria can be deadly when they enter a body, often through a scratch. MRSA spreads rapidly in hospitals where sick people are more vulnerable, but there have been outbreaks in prisons, gyms, even on beaches. When dormant, the bacteria are easily detected by a quick nasal swab and destroyed by antibiotics.

Dr. John Jernigan at the U.S. Centers for Disease Control and Prevention [CDC] said they incorporate some of Norway's solutions in varying degrees, and his agency "requires hospitals to move the needle, to show improvement, and if they don't show improvement they need to do more."

And if they don't?

"Nobody is accountable to our recommendations," he said, "but I assume hospitals and institutions are interested in doing the right thing."

Dr. Barry Farr, a retired epidemiologist who watched a successful MRSA control program launched 30 years ago at the University of Virginia's hospitals, blamed the CDC for clinging to past beliefs that hand washing is the best way to stop the spread of infections like MRSA. He says it's time to add screening and isolation methods to their controls.

## Success Stories

But can Norway's program really work elsewhere?

The answer lies in the busy laboratory of an aging little public hospital about 100 miles outside of London. It's here that microbiologist Dr. Lynne Liebowitz got tired of seeing the stunningly low Nordic MRSA rates while facing her own burgeoning cases.

So she turned Queen Elizabeth Hospital in King's Lynn into a petri dish, asking doctors to almost completely stop using two antibiotics known for provoking MRSA infections.

One month later, the results were in: MRSA rates were tumbling. And they've continued to plummet. Five years ago, the hospital had 47 MRSA bloodstream infections. This year they've had one.

"I was shocked, shocked," Liebowitz said.

When word spread of her success, Liebowitz's phone began to ring. So far she has replicated her experiment at four other hospitals, all with the same dramatic results.

"It's really very upsetting that some patients are dying from infections which could be prevented," she said. "It's wrong."

Around the world, various medical providers have also successfully adapted Norway's program with encouraging results. A medical center in Billings [Montana] cut MRSA infections by 89 percent by increasing screening, isolating patients and making all staff—not just doctors—responsible for increasing hygiene.

In 2001, the CDC approached a Veterans Affairs [VA] hospital in Pittsburgh [Pennsylvania] about conducting a small test program. It started in one unit, and within four years, the entire hospital was screening everyone who came through the door for MRSA. The result: an 80 percent decrease in MRSA infections. The program has now been expanded to all 153 VA hospitals, resulting in a 50 percent drop in MRSA bloodstream infections, said Dr. Robert Muder, chief of infectious diseases at the VA Pittsburgh Healthcare System.

"It's kind of a no-brainer," he said. "You save people pain, you save people the work of taking care of them, you save money, you save lives and you can export what you learn to other hospital-acquired infections."

> "Congress should create a number of economic incentives specifically designed to foster innovation in antibiotic development."

# MRSA Proliferates Because of the Failure to Develop New Antibiotics

*Barry Eisenstein*

*Barry Eisenstein is senior vice president for scientific affairs at Cubist Pharmaceuticals and a clinical professor of medicine at Harvard Medical School. In the following viewpoint, he argues that more new antibiotics are needed to fight drug-resistant bacteria. This problem is exacerbated, he says, by the fact that as antibiotics are used more carefully and less frequently, drug manufacturers have less incentive to develop them. He recommends that Congress set new guidelines for antibiotic use to reduce bacterial resistance, and create economic incentives to encourage drug manufacturers to invest more in developing new antibiotics.*

Barry Eisenstein, "Antibiotic Research, The Kryptonite of Superbugs," *Boston Globe*, October 19, 2009. Reproduced by permission of the author.

As you read, consider the following questions:

1. What percentage of staph infections were MRSA in 1980, and how much had that percentage increased by 2009, according to Eisenstein?

2. What does Eisenstein say that antibiotic stewardship programs should do?

3. Why does Eisenstein believe that Congress should extend the length of time during which a manufacturer has the right to be the sole producer of an antimicrobial product?

Hospital-acquired infections are a scourge that kill and injure patients and impose a heavy cost burden on the nation's health care system, so much so that policy makers are debating the idea of rewarding hospitals that reduce their infection rate and punishing those that don't. This makes sense, but it will not solve an important corollary public health crisis—the shortage of antibiotics to treat the current and the coming wave of superbugs.

## Infections Are More Resistant

The incidence of infections from drug-resistant bacteria such as MRSA (methicillin-resistant *Staphylococcus aureus*), commonly known as "staph" infection, continues to rise in hospitals and in community settings. In 1980, roughly 3 percent of staph infections were diagnosed as MRSA; today [2009] that number has reached 60 percent. The Centers for Disease Control and Prevention [CDC] reported that nearly 19,000 deaths were associated with MRSA in 2005. And in a disturbing new development, the CDC has reported evidence of a link between bacterial infections such as pneumonia caused by MRSA and the H1N1 virus [a virus strain that caused concern among public health officials in 2009] among patients who have died from the virus.

## Abandoning Antibiotic Research

In the past, large pharmaceutical companies were the primary sources of antibiotic research. But many of these companies have abandoned the field. "Eli Lilly and Company developed the first cephalosporins," [Harvard Medical School's Dr. Robert] Moellering told me, referring to familiar drugs like Keflex. "They developed a huge number of important antimicrobial agents. They had incredible chemistry and incredible research facilities, and, unfortunately, they have completely pulled out of it now. After Squibb merged with Bristol-Myers, they closed their antibacterial program," he said, as did Abbott [Laboratories].... A recent assessment of progress in the field, from UCLA [University of California, Los Angeles], concluded, "FDA approval of new antibacterial agents decreased by 56 percent over the past 20 years (1998–2002 vs. 1983–1987)," noting that, in the researchers' projection of future development only six of the 506 drugs currently being developed were new antibacterial agents. Drug companies are looking for blockbuster therapies that must be taken daily for decades, drugs like Lipitor, for high cholesterol, or Zyprexa, for psychiatric disorders, used by millions of people and generating many billions of dollars each year. Antibiotics are used to treat infections, and are therefore prescribed only for days or weeks.

*Jerome Groopman, "Superbugs,"*
New Yorker, *August 11, 2008. www.newyorker.com.*

While the incidence of MRSA rises, the treatment landscape is shrinking. Today, many of our antibiotic medications are not as effective as they once were. Every use of an antibiotic, including the widespread use of some for nontherapeutic purposes in livestock and poultry, increases the selection of naturally resistant bacteria, the rare bacteria that mutate to the resistant state, and the transfer of resistance genes to formerly susceptible pathogens. As these organisms survive and multiply over time, the once small number of resistant organisms becomes dominant, resulting in an increasingly dangerous number of drug-resistant bacteria.

In the face of the rising wave of drug-resistant bacteria, one would think that drug manufacturers would be busy trying to develop new antibiotics. Sadly, this is not the case. Right now, there are very few new antibiotics being developed in the United States or elsewhere. This dearth of new treatments was the subject of a recent report from the London School of Economics and Political Science. It warned that "only a handful of new antibiotics are in development, and all in the early stages."

## Encourage Antibiotic Development

What has brought us to this perilous situation? Since doctors now recognize the need to be prudent with antibiotic use, newly approved antibiotics do not have the commercial success they once might have had. As a consequence, drug manufacturers have abandoned antibiotic development in favor of more commercially reliable medications, particularly ones given for chronic [that is ongoing] (rather than acute) diseases.

To confront this crisis, Congress needs to take strong steps to increase the supply of new antibiotics. First, Congress should establish a federal anti-infective review board to guarantee antibiotics stewardship. Stewardship programs aim to ensure proper use of antibiotics in order to provide the best treatment outcomes, to lessen the risk of adverse effects (including antimicrobial resistance), and to promote cost-effectiveness. The review board would be responsible for compiling data on antibiotic use and setting guidelines, based on evidence-based medicine, for when certain drugs should be used or held.

Second, Congress should create a number of economic incentives specifically designed to foster innovation in antibiotic development. These incentives should include tax credits for research and development, which would enable manufacturers to take on the risks and costs associated with developing new treatments that otherwise may not be undertaken. These credits would also alleviate some of the hesitations manufacturers have about bringing a new product to market.

In the same context, Congress should extend the right of a manufacturer to be the sole producer of an antimicrobial product from the current five years to 10. Granting a manufacturer a longer period to offer a product increases the likelihood it can recoup its costs and in turn reinvest in delivering the next generation of antibiotics.

Taken together, these steps would help protect the current supply of antibiotics and encourage more drug developers to invest in this crucial area of research. This is not a matter of industry economics, but of having the ability to protect public health from the threat posed by the current and future wave of drug-resistant bacteria.

"We know that our environment affects our health to an enormous degree . . . and our microbiota are our most intimate environment by far."

# Widespread Use of Antibiotics May Cause Unexpected Health Problems

*Jessica Snyder Sachs*

*Jessica Snyder Sachs is a contributing editor to* Popular Science *and the author of* Good Germs, Bad Germs: Health and Survival in a Bacterial World. *In the following viewpoint, she reports that scientists are contemplating new uses for antibiotics, including using them to treat heart disease and arthritis. At the same time, she says, scientists fear that antibiotics may damage good bacteria that humans need and may be creating resistant bacteria that could cause dangerous infections. She concludes that greater use of antibiotics may result in unknown health problems in the future.*

As you read, consider the following questions:

1. How did Louis Pasteur and Élie Metchnikoff differ in their views of the usefulness of bacteria?

2. What role does the bacteria *B. theta* play in regulating the intestines, according to the researchers Sachs interviewed?

3. What is tetQ, and why did the researchers Sachs interviewed believe it was important?

Alan Hudson likes to tell a story about a soldier and his high school sweetheart.

## Hidden Infections

The young man returns from an overseas assignment for their wedding with a clean bill of health, having dutifully cleared up an infection of sexually transmitted chlamydia [a bacterial infection].

"Three weeks later, the wife has a screaming genital infection," Hudson recounts, "and I get a call from the small-town doctor who's trying to save their marriage." The soldier, it seems, has decided his wife must have been seeing other men, which she denies.

Hudson pauses for effect, stretching back in his seat and propping his feet on an open file drawer in a crowded corner of his microbiology laboratory at Wayne State [University] School [of Medicine] in Detroit. "The doctor is convinced she's telling the truth," he continues, folding his hands behind a sweep of white, collar-length hair. "So I tell him, 'Send me a specimen from him and a cervical swab from her.'" This is done after the couple has completed a full course of antibiotic treatment and tested free of infection.

"I PCR 'em both," Hudson says, "and he is red hot."

PCR stands for polymerase chain reaction—a technique developed about 20 years ago that allows many copies of a DNA sequence to be made. It is often used at crime scenes, where very little DNA may be available. Hudson's use of the technique allowed him to find traces of chlamydia DNA in the soldier and his wife that traditional tests miss because the amount left after antibiotic treatment is small and asymptomatic. Nonetheless, if a small number of inactive chlamydia cells passed from groom to bride, the infection could have become active in its new host.

Hudson tells the tale to illustrate how microbes that scientists once thought were easily eliminated by antibiotics can still thrive in the body. His findings and those of other researchers raise disturbing questions about the behavior of microbes in the human body and how they should be treated.

For example, Hudson has found that quiescent varieties of chlamydia may play a role in chronic ailments not traditionally thought to be related to this infectious agent. In the early 1990s, he found two types of chlamydia—*Chlamydia trachomatis* and *Chlamydia pneumoniae [C. pneumoniae]*—in the joint tissue of patients with inflammatory arthritis. More famously, in 1996, he began fishing *C. pneumonia* out of the brain cells of Alzheimer's [disease] victims. Since then, other researchers have made headlines after reporting the genetic fingerprints of *C. pneumonia*, as well as several kinds of common mouth bacteria, in the arterial plaque of heart attack patients. Hidden infections are now thought to be the basis of still other stubbornly elusive ills like chronic fatigue syndrome, Gulf War syndrome, multiple sclerosis, lupus, Parkinson's disease, and types of cancer.

To counteract these killers, some physicians have turned to lengthy or lifelong courses of antibiotics. At the same time, other researchers are counterintuitively finding that bacteria we think are bad for us also ward off other diseases and keep us healthy. Using antibiotics to tamper with this complicated and little-understood population could irrevocably alter the microbial ecology in an individual and accelerate the spread of drug-resistant genes to the public at large.

The two-faced puzzle regarding the role of bacteria is as old as the study of microbiology itself. Even as Louis Pasteur became the first to show that bacteria can cause disease, he assumed that bacteria normally found in the body are essential to life. Yet his protégé, Élie Metchnikoff, openly scoffed at the idea. Metchnikoff blamed indigenous bacteria for senility, atherosclerosis, and an altogether shortened life span—going even so far as to predict the day when surgeons would routinely remove the human colon simply to rid us of the "chronic poisoning" from its abundant flora.

Today we know that trillions of bacteria carpet not only our intestines but also our skin and much of our respiratory and urinary tracts. The vast majority of them seem to be innocuous, if not beneficial. And bacteria are everywhere, in abundances—they outnumber other cells in the human body by 10 to one. David Relman and his team at Stanford University and the VA [Veterans Affairs] Medical Center in Palo Alto, California, recently found the genetic fingerprints of several hundred new bacterial species in the mouths, stomachs, and intestines of healthy volunteers.

"What I hope," Relman says, "is that by starting with specimens from healthy people, the assumption would be that these microbes have probably been with us for some time relative to our stay on this planet and may, in fact, be important to our health."

Meanwhile, the behavior of even well-known bacterial inhabitants is challenging the old, straightforward view of infectious disease. In the 19th century, Robert Koch laid the foundation for medical microbiology, postulating: Any microorganism that causes a disease should be found in every case of the disease and always cause the disease when introduced into a new host. That view prevailed until the middle of this past century. Now we are more confused than ever. Take *Helicobacter pylori*. In the 1980s infection by the bacterium, not stress, was found to be the cause of most ulcers. Overnight, antibiotics became the standard treatment. Yet in the undeveloped world ulcers are rare, and *H. pylori* is pervasive.

"This stuff drives the old-time microbiologists mad," says Hudson, "because Koch's postulates simply don't apply." With new technologies like PCR, researchers are turning up stealth infections everywhere, yet they cause problems only in some people sometimes, often many years after the infection.

## Lifelong Antibiotics

These mysteries have nonetheless not stopped a free flow of prescriptions. Many rheumatologists, for example, now prescribe long-term—even lifelong—courses of antibiotics for inflammatory arthritis, even though it isn't known if the antibiotics actually clear away bacteria or reduce inflammatory arthritis in some other unknown manner.

Even more far-reaching is the use of antibiotics to treat heart disease, a trend that began in the early 1990s after studies associated *C. pneumonia* with the accumulation of plaque in arteries. In April [2005] large-scale studies reported that use of antibiotics does not reduce the incidence of heart attacks or eliminate *C. pneumonia*. But researchers left antibiotic-dosing cardiologists a strange option by admitting they do not know if stronger, longer courses of antibiotics or combined therapies would succeed.

Meanwhile, many researchers are alarmed. Infectious-diseases specialist Curtis Donskey, of Case Western Reserve University in Cleveland [Ohio], says: "Unfortunately, far too many physicians are still thinking of antibiotics as benign. We're just now beginning to understand how our normal microflora does such a good job of preventing our colonization by disease-causing microbes. And from an ecological point of view, we're just starting to understand the medical consequences of disturbing that with antibiotics."

Donskey has seen the problem firsthand at the Cleveland VA Medical Center, where he heads infection control. "Hospital patients get the broadest spectrum, most powerful antibiotics," he says, but they are also "in an environment where they get exposed to some of the nastiest, most drug-resistant pathogens." Powerful antibiotics can be dangerous in such a setting because they kill off harmless bacteria that create competition for drug-resistant colonizers, which can then proliferate. The result: Hospital-acquired infections have become a leading cause of death in critical care units.

"We also see serious problems in the outside community," Donskey says, because of inappropriate antibiotic use.

The consequences of disrupting the body's bacterial ecosystem can be minor, such as a yeast infection, or they can be major, such as the overgrowth of a relatively common gut bacterium called *Clostridium difficile*. A particularly nasty strain of *C. difficile* has killed hundreds of hospital patients in Canada over the past two years. Some had checked in for simple, routine procedures. The same strain is moving into hospitals in the United States and the United Kingdom.

## Helpful Bacteria

Jeffrey Gordon, a gastroenterologist turned full-time microbiologist, heads the spanking new Genome Center at Washington University in Saint Louis. The expansive, sun-streaked laboratory sits above the university's renowned gene-sequencing center, which proved a major player in powering the Human Genome Project. "Now it's time to take a broader view of the human genome," says Gordon, "one that recognizes that the human body probably contains 100 times more microbial genes than human ones."

Gordon supervises a lab of some 20 graduate students and postdocs [postdoctoral students] with expertise in disciplines ranging from ecology to crystallography. Their collaborations revolve around studies of unusually successful colonies of genetically engineered germ-free mice and zebra fish.

Gordon's veteran mouse wranglers, Marie Karlsson and her husband David O'Donnell, manage the rearing of germ-free animals for comparison with genetically identical animals that are colonized with one or two select strains of normal flora. In a cavernous facility packed with rows of crib-size bubble chambers, Karlsson and O'Donnell handle their germ-free charges via bulbous black gloves that serve as airtight portals into the pressurized isolettes. They generously supplement sterilized mouse chow with vitamins and extra calories to replace or complement what is normally supplied by intestinal bacteria. "Except for their being on the skinny side, we've got them to the point where they live near-normal lives," says O'Donnell. Yet the animals' intestines remain thin and underdeveloped in places, bizarrely bloated in others. They also prove vulnerable to any stray pathogen that slips into their food, water, or air.

All Gordon's protégés share an interest in following the molecular cross talk among resident microbes and their host when they add back a component of an animal's normal microbiota. One of the most interesting players is *Bacteroides thetaiotaomicron*, or *B. theta*, the predominant bacterium of the human colon and a particularly bossy symbiont.

The bacterium is known for its role in breaking down otherwise indigestible plant matter, providing up to 15 percent of its host's calories. But Gordon's team has identified a suite of other, more surprising skills. Three years ago, they sequenced *B. theta*'s entire genome, which enabled them to work with a gene chip that detects what proteins are being made at any given time. By tracking changes in the activity of these genes, the team has shown that *B. theta* helps guide the normal development and functioning of the intestines—including the growth of blood vessels, the proper turnover of epithelial cells, and the marshaling of components of the immune system needed to keep less well-behaved bacteria at bay. *B. theta* also exerts hormone-like, long-range effects that may help the host weather times when food is scarce and ensure the bacterium's own survival.

Fredrik Bäckhed, a young postdoc who came to Gordon's laboratory from the Karolinska Institute in Stockholm, has caught B. *theta* sending biochemical messages to host cells in the abdomen, directing them to store fat. When he gave germ-free mice an infusion of gut bacteria from a conventionally raised mouse, they immediately put on an average of 50 percent more fat although they were consuming 30 percent less food than when they were germ-free. "It's as if B. *theta* is telling its host, 'save this—we may need it later,'" Gordon says.

Justin Sonnenburg, another postdoctoral fellow, has documented that B. *theta* turns to the host's body for food when the animal stops eating. He has found that when a lab mouse misses its daily ration, B. *theta* consumes the globs of sugary mucus made every day by some cells in the intestinal lining. The bacteria graze on these platforms, which the laboratory has dubbed Whovilles (after the dust-speck metropolis of Dr. Seuss's *Horton Hears a Who!*). When the host resumes eating, B. *theta* returns to feeding on the incoming material.

Gordon's team is also looking at the ecological dynamics that take place when combinations of normal intestinal bacteria are introduced into germ-free animals. And he plans to study the dynamics in people by analyzing bacteria in fecal samples.

Among the questions driving him: Can we begin to use our microbiota as a marker of health and disease? Does this "bacterial nation" shift in makeup when we become obese, try to lose weight, experience prolonged stress, or simply age? Do people in Asia or Siberia harbor the same organisms in the same proportions as those in North America or the Andes?

"We know that our environment affects our health to an enormous degree," Gordon says. "And our microbiota are our most intimate environment by far."

## Superbugs in the Human Gut

A couple hundred miles northeast of Gordon's laboratory, microbiologist Abigail Salyers at the University of Illinois at Urbana-Champaign has been exploring a more sinister feature of our bacteria and their role in antibiotic resistance. At the center of her research stands a room-size, walk-in artificial "gut" with the thermostat set at the human intestinal temperature of 100.2 degrees Fahrenheit. Racks of bacteria-laced test tubes line three walls, the sealed vials purged of oxygen to simulate the anaerobic conditions inside a colon. Her study results are alarming.

Salyers says her research shows that decades of antibiotic use have bred a frightening degree of drug resistance into our intestinal flora. The resistance is harmless as long as the bacteria remain confined to their normal habitat. But it can prove deadly when those bacteria contaminate an open wound or cause an infection after surgery.

"Having a highly antibiotic-resistant bacterial population makes a person a ticking time bomb," says Salyers, who studies the genus *Bacteroides*, a group that includes not only *B. theta* but also about a quarter of the bacteria in the human gut. She has tracked dramatic increases in the prevalence of several genes and suites of genes, coding for drug resistance. She's particularly interested in tetQ a DNA sequence that conveys resistance to tetracycline drugs.

When her team tested fecal samples taken in the 1970s, they found that less than 25 percent of human-based *Bacteroides* carried tetQ. By the 1990s, that rate had passed the 85 percent mark, even among strains isolated from healthy people who hadn't used antibiotics in years. The dramatic uptick quashed hopes of reducing widespread antibiotic resistance by simply withdrawing or reducing the use of a given drug. Salyers's team also documented the spread of several *Bacteroides* genes conveying resistance to other antibiotics such as macrolides, which are widely used to treat skin, respiratory, genital, and blood infections.

As drug-resistant genes become common in bacteria in the gut, they are more likely to pass on their information to truly dangerous bugs that only move periodically through our bodies, says Salyers. Even distantly related bacteria can swap genes with one another using a variety of techniques, from direct cell-to-cell transfer, called conjugation, to transformation, in which a bacterium releases snippets of DNA that other bacteria pick up and use.

"Viewed in this way, the human colon is the bacterial equivalent of eBay," says Salyers. "Instead of creating a new gene the hard way—through mutation and natural selection—you can just stop by and obtain a resistance gene that has been created by some other bacterium."

Salyers has shown that *Bacteroides* probably picked up erythromycin-resistant genes from distantly related species of *Staphylococcus* and *Streptococcus*. Although neither bug colonizes the intestine, they are routinely inhaled and swallowed, providing a window of 24 to 48 hours in which they can commingle with intestinal flora before exiting. "That's more than long enough to pick up something interesting in the swinging singles bar of the human colon," she quips.

Most disturbing is Salyers's discovery that antibiotics like tetracycline actually stimulate *Bacteroides* to begin swapping its resistance genes. "If you think of the conjugative transfer of resistance genes as bacterial sex, you have to think of tetracycline as the aphrodisiac," she says. When Salyers exposes *Bacteroides* to other bacteria such as *Escherichia coli* under the disinhibiting influence of antibiotics, she has witnessed the step-by-step process by which the bacteria excise and transfer the tetQ gene from one species to another.

Nor is *Bacteroides* the only intestinal resident with such talents. "In June 2002, we passed a particularly frightening milestone," Salyers says. That summer, epidemiologists discovered hospital-bred strains of the gut bacterium *Enterococcus* harboring a gene that made them impervious to vancomycin. The bacterium may have since passed the gene to the far more dangerous *Staphylococcus aureus*, the most common cause of fatal surgical and wound infections.

"I am completely mystified by the lack of public concern about this problem," she says.

## Reduce Antibiotic Use, or Increase It?

With no simple solution in sight, Salyers continues to advise government agencies such as the Food and Drug Administration and the Department of Agriculture to reduce the use of antibiotics in livestock feed, a practice banned throughout the European Union. She supports the prescient efforts of Tufts University microbiologist Stuart Levy, founder of the Alliance for the Prudent Use of Antibiotics, which has been hectoring doctors to use antibiotics more judiciously.

Yet just when the message appears to be getting through—judging by a small but real reduction in antibiotic prescriptions—others are calling for an unprecedented increase in antibiotic use to clear the body of infections we never knew we had. Among them is William Mitchell, a Vanderbilt University chlamydia specialist. If antibiotics ever do prove effective for treating coronary artery disease, he says, the results would be "staggering. We're talking about the majority of the population being on long-term antibiotics, possibly multiple antibiotics."

Hudson cautions that before we set out to eradicate our bacterial fellow travelers, "we'd damn well better understand what they're doing in there." His interest centers on chlamydia, with its maddening ability to exist in inactive infections that flare into problems only for an unlucky few. Does the inactive form cause damage by secreting toxins or killing cells? Or is the real problem a disturbed immune response to them?

Lately Hudson has resorted to a device he once shunned in favor of DNA probes: a microscope, albeit an exotic $250,000 model. This instrument, which can magnify organisms an unprecedented 15,000 times, sits in the laboratory of Hudson's spouse, Judith Whittum-Hudson, a Wayne State immunologist who is working on a chlamydia vaccine. On a recent afternoon, Hudson marveled as a shimmering chlamydia cell was beginning to morph from its infectious stage into its mysterious and bizarre-looking persistent form. "One minute you have this perfectly normal, spherical bacterium and the next you have this big, goofy-looking doofus of a microbe," he says. He leans closer, focusing on a roiling spot of activity. "It's doing something. It's making something. It's saying something to its host."

# Periodical Bibliography

*The following articles have been selected to supplement the diverse views presented in this chapter.*

Nancy Amons — "MRSA Prevention Law Hopes to Save Lives," *WSMV Nashville Online*, April 22, 2010. www.wsmv.com.

Clive Cookson — "Scientists Develop New Antibiotic to Fight TB," *Financial Times*, March 21, 2010. www.ft.com.

Jerome Groopman — "Superbugs," *New Yorker*, August 11, 2008. www.newyorker.com.

Eben Harrell — "The Desperate Need for New Antibiotics," *Time*, October 1, 2009. www.time.com.

Nicholas D. Kristof — "The Spread of Superbugs," *New York Times*, March 6, 2010. www.nytimes.com.

Medical News Today — "Good Hygiene Is Key to Preventing MRSA," November 8, 2007. www.medicalnewstoday.com.

Medical News Today — "'Norway-Type' MRSA Strategy in U.S. Likely to Boost Diagnosis," January 22, 2010. www.medicalnewstoday.com.

Heidi Stevenson — "MRSA Superbug Nearly Nonexistent in Norway—Here's Why," Gaia Health, January 4, 2010. www.gaia-health.com.

Abigail Zuger — "Separating Friend from Foe Among the Body's Invaders," *New York Times*, November 27, 2007. www.nytimes.com.

# For Further Discussion

## Chapter 1

1. Ron Graves argues that methicillin-resistant *Staphylococcus aureus*, or MRSA, may be caused by medical practitioners' reluctance to prescribe antibiotics quickly enough or in large enough doses. This contradicts Zachary Meisel. Who do you think is a better source in regards to this issue: Graves or those arguing against him? Explain your answer.

## Chapter 2

1. The Ohio Pork Producers Council says that the answer to the question of whether antibiotic usage has decreased in Denmark is "yes and no." What does the viewpoint mean by this? Is this a fair characterization of the facts? Based on this viewpoint and the viewpoint by the Pew Charitable Trusts, would you say that Denmark has or has not reduced antibiotic usage?

2. Matthew Cimitile argues that antibiotics in vegetables may be dangerous. Martin Hickman and Genevieve Roberts report that many in Europe worry about the dangers of genetically modified potatoes. Does either of these viewpoints provide any evidence that the affected plants are in fact dangerous for humans to eat? Might their fears be justified even if no evidence exists? Explain your answer.

## Chapter 3

1. Raphael B. Stricker argues that antibiotic treatment has sometimes failed in cases of Lyme disease. Edward McSweegan argues that this is not the case. What evidence does Stricker present for his view? What evidence does McSweegan present for his view? Whose argument do you find more convincing?

2. What kind of emotional arguments does Stewart Baker make in arguing that the U.S. Postal Service will not do a good job of delivering antibiotics in case of an emergency? Are these arguments convincing? Do the dangers Baker discusses seem more or less convincing to you than the dangers in stockpiling antibiotics that David Malakoff discusses?

## Chapter 4

1. Steven Milloy has a number of criticisms of the study on breast cancer and antibiotics conducted by the National Cancer Institute. He says, "No evidence was presented that antibiotics were the biological cause of any of the cases of breast cancer considered in the study." Does the National Cancer Institute claim to have any such evidence? What other criticisms does Milloy make, and does the National Cancer Institute provide responses to any of them?

2. Martha Mendoza and Margie Mason suggest one approach to fighting methicillin-resistant *Staphylococcus aureus* (MRSA); Barry Eisenstein suggests another. Are these solutions mutually exclusive? Which solution do you think would be more expensive? Which seems like it would be more effective?

# Organizations to Contact

*The editors have compiled the following list of organizations concerned with the issues presented in this book. The descriptions are derived from materials provided by the organizations. All have publications or information available for interested readers. The list was compiled on the date of publication of the present volume; the information provided here may change. Be aware that many organizations take several weeks or longer to respond to inquiries, so allow as much time as possible.*

**Alliance for the Prudent Use of Antibiotics (APUA)**
75 Kneeland Street, Boston, MA  02111-1901
(617) 636-0966 • fax: (617) 636-3999
e-mail: apua@tufts.edu
Web site: www.tufts.edu/med/apua

Alliance for the Prudent Use of Antibiotics (APUA) is a non-profit organization with chapters in more than sixty countries. It is dedicated to containing antibiotic resistance and improving antibiotic effectiveness through research, education, capacity building, and global and grassroots advocacy. APUA's Web site contains research reports, copies of advocacy letters, meeting reports, and references. APUA publishes the quarterly *APUA* newsletter.

**Center for Agricultural and Rural Development (CARD)**
Iowa State University, 578 Heady Hall, Ames, IA  50011-1070
(515) 294-1183 • fax: (515) 294-6336
Web site: www.card.iastate.edu/

Center for Agricultural and Rural Development (CARD) is an academic organization connected to Iowa State University that conducts public policy and economic research on agricultural, environmental, and food issues. Its Web site includes numerous articles on antibiotic use in agriculture, such as "What Would Happen if Over-the-Counter Antibiotics Were Banned (in Swine Rations)?" It also publishes the quarterly *Iowa Ag Review.*

## Centers for Disease Control and Prevention (CDC)

1600 Clifton Road, Atlanta, GA   30333
(800) 232-4636
Web site: www.cdc.gov

The Centers for Disease Control and Prevention (CDC), founded in 1946, was originally charged with the task of finding methods to control malaria. Since its inception, the organization's mission has broadened, but it still focuses on preventing and managing both communicable and noncommunicable diseases. The CDC offers guidelines for professionals and the general public on how to behave to slow or prevent the spread of infectious diseases. The organization also provides many fact sheets and articles on antibiotic use and preventing the development of resistant bacteria strains. Two journals published by the CDC are *Emerging Infectious Diseases* and *Preventing Chronic Disease.*

## Infectious Diseases Society of America (IDSA)

1300 Wilson Boulevard, Suite 300, Arlington, VA   22209
(703) 299-0200 • fax: (702) 299-0204
e-mail: info@idsociety.org
Web site: www.idsociety.org

The Infectious Diseases Society of America (IDSA) is an organization of health care and scientific professionals concerned with the prevention and treatment of infectious diseases. The society provides research suggesting how to provide the best care for individuals with communicable diseases. The IDSA also works as an advocacy group promoting sound public policy on infectious diseases. IDSA's Web site includes many resources focused on antibiotics, including "Key Studies to Answer Basic Antibiotics Questions" and "Final Report of the

Lyme Disease Review Panel of IDSA." In addition to the *IDSA News*, the society publishes the journals *Clinical Infectious Diseases* and *Journal of Infectious Diseases.*

## Mayo Clinic
13400 East Shea Boulevard, Scottsdale, AZ    85259
(480) 301-8000 • fax: (480) 301-7006
Web site: www.mayoclinic.org

Mayo Clinic is a not-for-profit medical practice, medical research group, and medical school with locations in Minnesota, Arizona, and Florida. Besides delivering health care, part of its mission includes education and outreach. To fulfill that goal, it has established MayoClinic.com, a Web site that includes extensive information about numerous health conditions and treatments. The site has many articles on antibiotic issues, including "Antibiotics and Alcohol: Should I Avoid Mixing Them?" and "Antibiotics: Misuse Puts You and Others at Risk."

## The Road Back Foundation (RBF)
PO Box 410184, Cambridge, MA    02141
(614) 227-1556
e-mail: rbfcontact@roadback.org
Web site: www.roadback.org

The Road Back Foundation (RBF) provides information about and advocacy for antibiotic treatment for rheumatic disease. RBF's Web site includes a downloadable brochure, lists of studies, and numerous articles such as "A Conceptual View of Antibiotic Therapy" and "Antibiotic Therapy for Rheumatic Disease: Routes of Administration."

## U.S. Department of Agriculture (USDA)
1400 Independence Avenue SW, Washington, DC    20250
(202) 720-2791
Web site: www.usda.gov

The U.S. Department of Agriculture (USDA) is the government department responsible for developing and executing U.S. farm policy. Its Web site includes news updates, reports, and publications such as *Agriculture Fact Book*. The Web site also provides access to many articles about antibiotic use in agriculture such as "Antibiotic Use on U.S. Dairy Operations, 2002 and 2007."

## U.S. Department of Health & Human Services (HHS)
200 Independence Avenue SW, Washington, DC   20201
(877) 696-6775
Web site: www.hhs.gov

U.S. Department of Health & Human Services (HHS) is the government department that concentrates on the public's health and well-being. HHS is the parent agency of other government health organizations such as the Centers for Disease Control (CDC) and the National Institutes of Health (NIH). Among the department's many services, disease prevention is a top priority. HHS manages many services dedicated to researching new options to combat disease and creating informative programs for the public. The department's Web site includes numerous documents relating to antibiotics, including fact sheets, news reports, transcripts of Senate testimony, and more.

## U.S. Food and Drug Administration (FDA)
10903 New Hampshire Avenue,
Silver Spring, MD   20993-0002
(888) 463-6332
Web site: www.fda.gov

The U.S. Food and Drug Administration (FDA) is part of the U.S. Department of Health & Human Services (HHS) and is responsible for the regulation and supervision of food safety and of medications. The FDA's Web site includes many reports and articles about antibiotic use, such as "Antibiotics and Antibiotic Resistance," as well as congressional testimony.

## World Health Organization (WHO)
Avenue Appia 20,
Geneva 27   CH-1211 Switzerland
+41 22 791 21 11 • fax: + 41 22 791 31 11

e-mail: info@who.int
Web site: www.who.int

The World Health Organization (WHO) is an agency of the United Nations formed in 1948 with the goal of creating and ensuring a world in which all people can live with high levels of both mental and physical health. The organization researches and endorses different methods of using antibiotics to combat diseases, such as tuberculosis, and of monitoring antibiotic resistance. The WHO publishes the *Bulletin of the World Health Organization*, which is available online, and the *Pan American Journal of Public Health*. Within the WHO, the Pan American Health Organization (PAHO) is the regional office that covers the United States.

# Bibliography of Books

Kevin Brown — *Penicillin Man: Alexander Fleming and the Antibiotic Revolution.* Stroud, Gloucestershire, UK: Sutton, 2005.

William R. Clark — *Bracing for Armageddon? The Science and Politics of Bioterrorism in America.* New York: Oxford University Press, 2008.

John D. Clough — *The Cleveland Clinic Guide to Arthritis.* New York: Kaplan Publishing, 2009.

Dorothy H. Crawford — *Deadly Companions: How Microbes Shaped Our History.* New York: Oxford University Press, 2009.

Madeline Drexler — *Emerging Epidemics: The Menace of New Infections.* New York: Penguin, 2003.

Jason C. Gallagher and Conan MacDougall — *Antibiotics, Simplified.* Sudbury, MA: Jones and Bartlett Publishers, 2009.

Pat Ganger and Carol Lange — *Solving the Puzzling Problem of Arthritis: An Antibiotic Treatment Handbook for Patients and Doctors.* Columbus, OH: Gom MedPress, 2004.

David Kirby — *Animal Factory: The Looming Threat of Industrial Pig, Dairy, and Poultry Farms to Humans and the*

*Environment.* New York: St. Martin's Press, 2010.

| | |
|---|---|
| Lynn C. Klotz and Edward J. Sylvester | *Breeding Bio Insecurity: How U.S. Biodefense Is Exporting Fear, Globalizing Risk, and Making Us All Less Secure.* Chicago, IL: The University of Chicago Press, 2009. |
| Tim Lang and Michael Heasman | *Food Wars: The Global Battle for Mouths, Minds, and Markets.* London, UK: Earthscan, 2004. |
| Stuart B. Levy | *The Antibiotic Paradox: How the Misuse of Antibiotics Destroys Their Curative Power.* Cambridge, MA: Perseus, 2002. |
| Maryn McKenna | *Superbug: The Fatal Menace of MRSA.* New York: Free Press, 2010. |
| Peter Pringle | *Food, Inc.: Mendel to Monsanto—The Promises and Perils of the Biotech Harvest.* New York: Simon & Schuster, 2003. |
| L.A. Reynolds and E.M. Tansey, eds. | *Superbugs and Superdrugs: A History of MRSA.* London, UK: Wellcome Trust Centre for the History of Medicine at UCL, 2008. |
| Jessica Snyder Sachs | *Good Germs, Bad Germs: Health and Survival in a Bacterial World.* New York: Hill and Wang, 2007. |
| Abigail A. Salyers and Dixie D. Whitt | *Revenge of the Microbes: How Bacterial Resistance Is Undermining the Antibiotic Miracle.* Washington, DC: ASM Press, 2005. |

| Michael A. Schmidt | *Beyond Antibiotics: Strategies for Living in a World of Emerging Infections and Antibiotic-Resistant Bacteria.* Berkeley, CA: North Atlantic Books, 2009. |
|---|---|
| Michael Shnayerson and Mark J. Plotkin | *The Killers Within: The Deadly Rise of Drug-Resistant Bacteria.* New York: Little, Brown and Company, 2002. |
| Jeffrey M. Smith | *Genetic Roulette: The Documented Health Risks of Genetically Engineered Foods.* White River Junction, VT: Chelsea Green, 2007. |
| Brad Spellberg | *Rising Plague: The Global Threat from Deadly Bacteria and Our Dwindling Arsenal to Fight Them.* Amherst, NY: Prometheus Books, 2009. |
| Tanya Stivers | *Prescribing Under Pressure: Parent-Physician Conversations and Antibiotics.* New York: Oxford University Press, 2007. |
| Karen Vanderhoof-Forschner | *Everything You Need to Know About Lyme Disease and Other Tick-Borne Disorders.* 2nd ed. Hoboken, NJ: John Wiley & Sons, 2003. |

# Index

**F**

**G**